United States Government Accountability Office

Report to the Chairman, Committee on Homeland Security and Governmental Affairs, U.S. Senate

September 2014

DHS TRAINING

Improved Documentation, Resource Tracking, and Performance Measurement Could Strengthen Efforts

GAO-14-688

Highlights of GAO-14-688, a report to the Chairman, Committee on Homeland Security and Governmental Affairs, U.S. Senate

September 2014

DHS TRAINING

Improved Documentation, Resource Tracking, and Performance Measurement Could Strengthen Efforts

Why GAO Did This Study

DHS is the third-largest cabinet-level department in the federal government, with over 230,000 employees doing diverse jobs. To fulfill its complex mission, DHS's workforce must have the necessary skills and expertise. GAO previously reported on DHS's hiring and recruiting efforts. GAO was asked to assess DHS's training practices.

This report addresses (1) the extent to which DHS has documented processes to evaluate training and reliably capture costs and (2) the extent to which DHS measures the performance of its leader development programs. To conduct its work, GAO reviewed documented training evaluation processes, training cost data from fiscal year 2011 through fiscal year 2013, and leadership training programs. GAO also interviewed training officials at the department level and at the five DHS components selected for this review about their varieties of training and development programs. Information from these components cannot be generalized to all of DHS, but provides insights.

What GAO Recommends

GAO recommends that DHS update its documentation to fully reflect key attributes of an effective evaluation, identify challenges to and corrective measures for capturing training costs department-wide, and clearly identify LDP goals and ensure that LDP performance measures reflect key attributes. DHS concurred and identified actions to address our recommendations.

View GAO-14-688. For more information, contact David C. Maurer at (202) 512-9627 or maurerd@gao.gov.

What GAO Found

The Department of Homeland Security (DHS) has processes to evaluate training, track resources, and assess leader development. However, various actions could better position the department to maximize the impact of its training efforts.

Training evaluation: All five DHS components in GAO's review—U.S. Customs and Border Protection, U.S. Immigration and Customs Enforcement, the U.S. Coast Guard, the Transportation Security Administration, and the Federal Law Enforcement Training Center—have a documented process to evaluate their training programs. Their documented processes fully included three of six attributes of effective training evaluation processes identifying goals, programs to evaluate, and how results are to be used. However, the documented processes did not consistently include the other three attributes: methodology, timeframes, and roles and responsibilities (see table). By updating documentation to address these attributes, DHS components would have more complete information to guide its efforts in conducting effective evaluations.

Summary of Training Evaluation Attributes DHS Could Better Document

	Customs and Border Protection	U.S. Coast Guard	Immigration and Customs Enforcement	Transportation Security Administration	Federal Law Enforcement Training Center
Methodology	◗	●	●	◗	◗
Timeframes	◗	◗	●	◗	●
Roles and responsibilities	◗	●	◗	◗	●

●: Documented evaluation processes fully included information to meet the attribute.

◗: Documented evaluation processes partly included some information to address a given attribute.

Source: GAO analysis of documented evaluation processes. I GAO-14-688

Capturing training cost: DHS identified efficiencies and cost savings for delivering a number of training programs. However, different methods are used for capturing training costs across the department, which poses challenges for reliably capturing these costs across DHS. Components capture training costs differently, contributing to inconsistencies in training costs captured across DHS. Variation in methods used to collect data can affect the reliability and quality of DHS-wide training program costs. However, DHS has not identified all challenges that contribute to these inconsistencies. DHS could improve its awareness about the costs of training programs DHS-wide and thereby enhance its resource stewardship by identifying existing challenges that prevent DHS from accurately capturing training costs and implementing corrective measures.

Leader development: DHS's Leader Development Program (LDP) Office is in the process of implementing a department-wide framework to build leadership skills. However, the LDP Office has not clearly identified program goals and the measures it uses to assess program effectiveness do not exhibit some attributes that GAO previously identified as key for successful performance measurement. These include linkage of performance measures to the program's goals, clarity, and establishment of measurable targets to assess the measures. By clearly identifying program goals and incorporating key attributes, the LDP could better ensure actionable information for identifying and making program improvements.

_____ United States Government Accountability Office

Contents

Figures

Abbreviations

CBP	U.S. Customs and Border Protection
CITP	Criminal Investigator Training Program
DFOTP	ICE D Field Operations Training Program
DHS	Department of Homeland Security
EAB	Evaluation and Analysis Branch
ECQ	Executive Core Qualification
FEVS	Federal Employee Viewpoint Survey
FLETA	Federal Law Enforcement Training Accreditation
FLETC	Federal Law Enforcement Training Center
ICE	U.S. Immigration and Customs Enforcement
LDP	Leader Development Program
OCHCO	Office of the Chief Human Capital Officer
OPM	Office of Personnel Management
OTWE	Office of Training and Workforce Engagement
PWCS	Ports, Waterways Coastal Security
SES	Senior Executive Service
SOP	standard operating procedures
SSI	Sensitive Security Information
TLC	Training Leaders Council
TSA	Transportation Security Administration
TSO	transportation security officer

441 G St. N.W.
Washington, DC 20548

September 10, 2014

The Honorable Thomas R. Carper
Chairman
Committee on Homeland Security and Governmental Affairs
United States Senate

Dear Mr. Chairman:

The Department of Homeland Security (DHS) is the third-largest cabinet-level department in the federal government, with over 230,000 employees doing diverse jobs in areas such as aviation, border security, emergency response, cybersecurity analysis, and chemical facility inspection. To address increasingly complex national security challenges, it is important that DHS have a workforce with the skills and expertise to fulfill its mission.[1] Training and development programs are one way to help ensure personnel have the necessary skills and to prevent competency gaps.[2] These programs can include a set of courses using a variety of approaches, including classroom training, e-learning, webinars, coaching, practical exercises, and rotational assignments. Effective training and development programs for DHS's mission-critical functions, such as law enforcement, inspections, and screening, are important for enhancing DHS's ability to retain employees with the skills and competencies needed to achieve results.[3] According to DHS officials, DHS spent about $1.1 billion on training and development programs in fiscal year 2012 and

---

[1]GAO, *DHS Recruiting and Hiring: DHS Is Generally Filling Mission-Critical Positions, but Could Better Track Costs of Coordinated Recruiting Efforts*, GAO-13-742 (Washington, D.C.: Sept. 17, 2013).

[2]In previous GAO reports we defined "training" as making available to employees planned and coordinated educational programs of instruction in professional, technical, or other fields that are or will be related to their job responsibilities. Similarly, we defined "development" to generally include aspects of training, as well as structured on-the-job learning experiences (such as coaching, mentoring, or rotational assignments) and education. For the purposes of this report, "training" will be used as a shorter substitute for "training and development."

[3]Selected components defined "mission-critical training" to include those training programs that most directly affect a component's ability to perform its mission.

about 7,000 staff are dedicated to training and development activities across the department.[4]

In addition, our work in identifying high-risk areas in the federal government has identified DHS management, including the function of human capital management, as a high-risk area. DHS's management of human capital has been on our high-risk list since 2003 because, among other things, the department has not fully implemented a mechanism to assess education, training, and other development programs and opportunities to help employees build and acquire needed skills and competencies.[5] In addition, our high-risk work has also identified the need for DHS to improve employees' opinions of the quality of departmental leadership as reflected in DHS's scores on the Office of Personnel Management's (OPM) Federal Employee Viewpoint Survey.[6] DHS uses training as one of its tools for enhancing departmental leadership. As we have reported since March 2004, using training evaluations to demonstrate how training efforts help develop employees, improve agencies' performance, and inform decision making on investments in training is a leading practice for ensuring agencies are being good stewards of their training and development resources.[7]

Given today's fiscal realities and the need to deliver cost-effective training and development programs without sacrificing quality or training effectiveness, you asked us to evaluate DHS's training practices, as well as efforts to ensure training is efficient and effective in developing its next cadre of leaders. This report will address the following two questions.

---

[4]Fiscal year 2012 is the most recent year for which DHS data for training and development program costs across the department are available.

[5]GAO, *High-Risk Series: An Update*, GAO-13-283 (Washington, D.C.: Feb. 14, 2013).

[6]The Federal Employee Viewpoint Survey is a tool that measures employees' perceptions of whether and to what extent conditions characterizing successful organizations are present in their agency. As we reported in December 2013, DHS has consistently scored lower than the government-wide average on the survey's Leadership and Knowledge Management Index, which indicates the extent to which employees hold their leadership in high regard both overall and on specific facets of leadership. See GAO, *Department of Homeland Security: DHS's Efforts to Improve Employee Morale and Fill Senior Leadership Vacancies*, GAO-14-228T (Washington, D.C.: Dec. 12, 2013).

[7]GAO, *Human Capital: A Guide for Assessing Strategic Training and Development Efforts in the Federal Government*, GAO-04-546G (Washington, D.C.: March 2004).

1. To what extent does DHS have documented processes to evaluate training and development programs and reliably capture costs?

2. What leader development programs has DHS implemented, what are stakeholders' perspectives on them, and to what extent does DHS measure program performance?

To understand training programs at DHS, we obtained information from the DHS Office of the Chief Human Capital Officer (OCHCO), and five selected components: the Federal Law Enforcement Training Center (FLETC), U.S. Customs and Border Protection (CBP), U.S. Immigration and Customs Enforcement (ICE), the Transportation Security Administration (TSA), and the U.S. Coast Guard. We selected these components to represent different DHS mission areas, workforce sizes, training costs, and number of career Senior Executive Service (SES) personnel. To further our understanding of training at the component level, we also interviewed training officials at each of the selected components and identified these individuals based on their knowledge, experience, and leadership roles. The perspectives of DHS OCHCO and the selected components provided are not generalizable to all training programs at DHS, but provided helpful insights into the selected components' specific training and development programs at DHS.

To address the first question regarding the extent to which DHS has documented processes to evaluate its training and development programs, we reviewed documented policies and procedures related to the evaluation of training programs for the five selected DHS components, as well as completed training evaluations. We also conducted semistructured interviews with officials responsible for conducting training evaluation at each of the five components to understand the evaluation process that each component follows and how evaluation feedback is used.[8] We then assessed the documented processes from each of the selected components against attributes of training evaluation processes identified by OPM, DHS, and GAO to determine the extent to which the documents include select attributes of evaluation processes. We selected the attributes for our analysis by including six that were consistently identified in relevant criteria documents related to training evaluation, such as the *DHS Learning*

---

[8]During this review, we asked components to identify the training programs that they define as mission-critical. For example, ICE defines a program as mission-critical when the completion of a training program is required as a condition of employment.

Evaluation Guide,[9] the OPM *Training Evaluation Field Guide,*[10] and GAO's prior work on training and development.[11] These attributes also align with those identified in *Standards for Internal Control in the Federal Government* for the plans, methods, and procedures used to accomplish missions, goals, and objectives and support performance-based management practices.[12] The six training evaluation process attributes include assessing whether each component's documented process (1) establishes goals about what the training program is supposed to achieve, (2) indicates which training programs are being evaluated, (3) explains the methodology used to conduct the evaluation, (4) presents timeframes for conducting the evaluation, (5) presents roles and responsibilities for evaluation efforts, and (6) explains how the evaluation results will be used. We assessed each component's documented evaluation process to determine the extent to which the attributes were included and gave a component a rating indicating that the attribute was fully met, a component partially met the attribute but did not fully or consistently meet all parts, or the component did not include any information to meet the attribute.

To address the extent to which DHS ensures training costs are reliably captured, we reviewed relevant documentation on processes and steps taken to examine budget and cost documentation. As part of our review of cost tracking at DHS, we observed methods OCHCO and the components used for identifying efficiencies in training that were used to identify cost savings. We also conducted semistructured interviews with DHS and component officials responsible for administering training programs and tracking costs to understand how DHS and components identified and captured costs, and any challenges they may have in doing so in a reliable manner. Accordingly, through our review of cost-saving documentation and interviews with DHS and component officials, we sought illustrative examples to understand how OCHCO and the selected DHS components identified potential efficiencies and steps planned or

---

[9]DHS, *DHS Learning Evaluation Guide* (Washington, D.C.: October 2010).

[10]OPM, *Training Evaluation Field Guide: Demonstrating the Value of Training at Every Level,* (Washington, D.C.: January 2011).

[11]GAO-04-546G.

[12]GAO, *Standards for Internal Control in the Federal Government* (Washington, D.C.: Nov. 1, 1999).

already taken to achieve them. We assessed the reliability of the reported cost savings relevant to these illustrative examples and we replicated cost-saving calculations provided by components, including estimates for training equipment, salaries, and benefits. We determined through analysis of cost-saving estimates and interviews with knowledgeable officials at DHS and the select components that the cost-saving data provided and reported in this product for the illustrative examples from fiscal years 2011 through 2013 were sufficiently reliable for the purposes of illustrating the types of cost efficiencies that may be achieved. The cost-saving examples DHS and components provided are not generalizable to all of DHS, but provided helpful insights into cost-saving efforts identified to date at DHS.

To address the second question about leader development programs DHS has implemented, we reviewed program documentation relevant to leadership training programs. In addition, we obtained and analyzed data from OCHCO and the selected components on the number of participants in the leader development programs they provided during fiscal years 2012 and 2013.[13] We assessed the reliability of these data by interviewing agency officials familiar with the sources of the data regarding internal controls built into the information systems and stand-alone spreadsheets in which the data are stored, and quality assurance steps performed after data are entered into the systems or documents. We determined that the data were sufficiently reliable for the purpose of reporting the approximate number of program participants. We also interviewed officials from OCHCO and the selected components regarding implemented and planned leader development programs. To assess the extent to which DHS measures the performance of leader development programs, we reviewed program documentation from OCHCO and the selected components, including performance measurement requirements and guidance. In addition, we interviewed cognizant officials about what performance measurement information they collect and how they use the information. Through these efforts we determined that the Leader Development Program (LDP) Office uses performance measures to assess the LDP's impact. We assessed these measures against three of nine selected key attributes for performance measures identified in prior GAO work that we identified as relevant given

---

[13]We selected this time frame in order to focus on the most current leader development programs DHS provides. Fiscal year 2013 was the most recent year for which complete data were available at the time of our review.

the maturity level of the LDP.[14] In particular, given that the LDP is a relatively new program, we focused our analysis on three attributes that we identified as foundational—having linkage between performance measures and division- and agency-wide goals, being clear, and having measurable targets. Additional details on our scope and methodology can be found in appendix I.

We conducted this performance audit from July 2013 to September 2014, in accordance with generally accepted government auditing standards. Those standards require that we plan and perform the audit to obtain sufficient, appropriate evidence to provide a reasonable basis for our findings and conclusions based on our audit objectives. We believe that the evidence obtained provides a reasonable basis for our findings and conclusions based on our audit objectives.

Background

DHS Training and Development Roles and Responsibilities

DHS's OCHCO is responsible, in broad terms, for the strategy, oversight, and planning of DHS employee training and development. At the same time, each DHS component, such as CBP and TSA, also has its own human capital office and training and development functions. In practice, DHS's OCHCO focuses on department-wide efforts while each component focuses on ensuring its employees are trained and developed to meet its specific mission needs. In addition, FLETC, a component of DHS, offers and delivers law enforcement training to DHS components, including those in our review—CBP, ICE, TSA, and the Coast Guard. FLETC also serves as an interagency law enforcement training organization for more than 90 federal partner organizations, as well as state, local, tribal, and international entities. Table 1 provides a summary

---

[14]GAO, *Tax Administration: IRS Needs to Further Refine Its Tax Filing Season Performance Measures*, GAO-03-143 (Washington, D.C.: Nov. 22, 2002).GAO developed these nine attributes of performance goals and measures based on previously established GAO criteria, consideration of key legislation, and review of performance management literature. In GAO-03-143, GAO applied the attributes to assess Internal Revenue Service performance measures. However, because the attributes are derived from sources generally applicable to performance measures, they are also relevant for assessing LDP performance measures.

of training and development responsibilities at OCHCO and DHS components selected for our review.

Table 1: Summary of Training and Development Responsibilities at Department of Homeland Security and Selected Components

DHS and selected components	Training and development responsibilities
Department of Homeland Security (DHS)	The Office of the Chief Human Capital Officer (OCHCO) is responsible for DHS-wide strategy and policy on human capital issues, including the oversight, planning, and training of employees. For example, OCHCO is also responsible for delivering department-wide select mandatory training courses and implementing a leader development framework through the Leader Development Program.
U.S. Customs and Border Protection (CBP)	CBP's Office of Training and Development is responsible for designing, developing, delivering, and evaluating CBP-wide training courses and establishing training standards and policies.
Federal Law Enforcement Training Center (FLETC)	FLETC provides interagency law enforcement-specific training to several DHS components and provides a venue for many of the DHS components and other federal agencies' training academies.[a]
Immigration and Customs Enforcement (ICE)	ICE's Office of Training and Development is responsible for designing, developing, delivering, and evaluating ICE-wide training courses. ICE's Office of Firearms and Tactical Programs delivers training related to the use of force; ICE also provides specialized training for discrete segments of the ICE workforce.
Transportation Security Administration (TSA)	TSA's Office of Training and Workforce Engagement is responsible for standardizing and integrating the development and delivery of TSA training, employee development, and workforce engagement programs.
U.S. Coast Guard	The Coast Guard's Force Readiness Command is responsible for establishing component-wide training standards and policies and supervising each of the training centers. Coast Guard program offices request the training programs that are provided at the Coast Guard's training centers nationwide.

Source: GAO analysis of DHS roles and responsibilities. I GAO-14-688

[a]FLETC provides law enforcement training to federal, state, local, tr bal and international entities. FLETC has provided law enforcement training to each of the four other DHS components in our review: CBP, ICE, TSA, and the Coast Guard.

Overview of Training Evaluation Requirements and Evaluation Models

In 2009, OPM developed and published regulations that require agencies to regularly evaluate training programs.[15] Among other things, these regulations require agencies to evaluate their training programs annually to determine how well such plans and programs contribute to mission accomplishment and meet organizational performance goals.

---

[15]5 C.F.R. § 410.202. Under the Aviation and Transportation Security Act, TSA is generally exempt from the provisions of Title 5 of the U.S. Code as well as the policies and procedures OPM established under Title 5, in order to adapt processes to align with the unique demands of the agency's workforce. See 49 U.S.C. § 114(n). Nevertheless, TSA has an evaluation process in place.

The training and development process can loosely be segmented into four broad, interrelated elements: (1) planning/front-end analysis, (2) design/development, (3) implementation, and (4) evaluation. The four elements help to produce a strategic approach to federal agencies' training and development efforts. One commonly accepted training evaluation model, which is endorsed by OPM in its training evaluation guidance, is known as the Kirkpatrick model. This model is commonly used in the federal government, including at DHS. The Kirkpatrick model consists of a four-level approach for soliciting feedback from training course participants and evaluating the impact the training had on individual development, among other things.[16] The following is a description of what each level within the Kirkpatrick model is to accomplish:

- Level 1: The first level measures the training participants' reaction to, and satisfaction with, the training program. A level 1 evaluation could take the form of a course survey that a participant fills out immediately after completing the training.
- Level 2: The second level measures the extent to which learning has occurred because of the training effort. A level 2 evaluation could take the form of a written exam that a participant takes during the course.
- Level 3: The third level measures how training affects changes in behavior on the job. Such an evaluation could take the form of a survey sent to participants several months after they have completed the training to follow up on the impact of the training on the job.
- Level 4: The fourth level measures the impact of the training program on the agency's mission or organizational results. Such an evaluation could take the form of comparing operational data before and after a training modification was made. Figure 1 highlights the elements of the training development process, from the planning stage through the implementation and evaluation of training, and depicts how the Kirkpatrick model complements the training development process.

---

[16]Donald L. Kirkpatrick (author of *Evaluating Training Programs: The Four Levels,* third edition (San Francisco, California: Berrett-Koehler Publishers, Inc. 2012) developed a four-level model for evaluating training and development efforts. The fourth level is sometimes split into two levels with the fifth level representing a comparison of costs and benefits quantified in dollars.

Figure 1: The Components of the Training Development Process

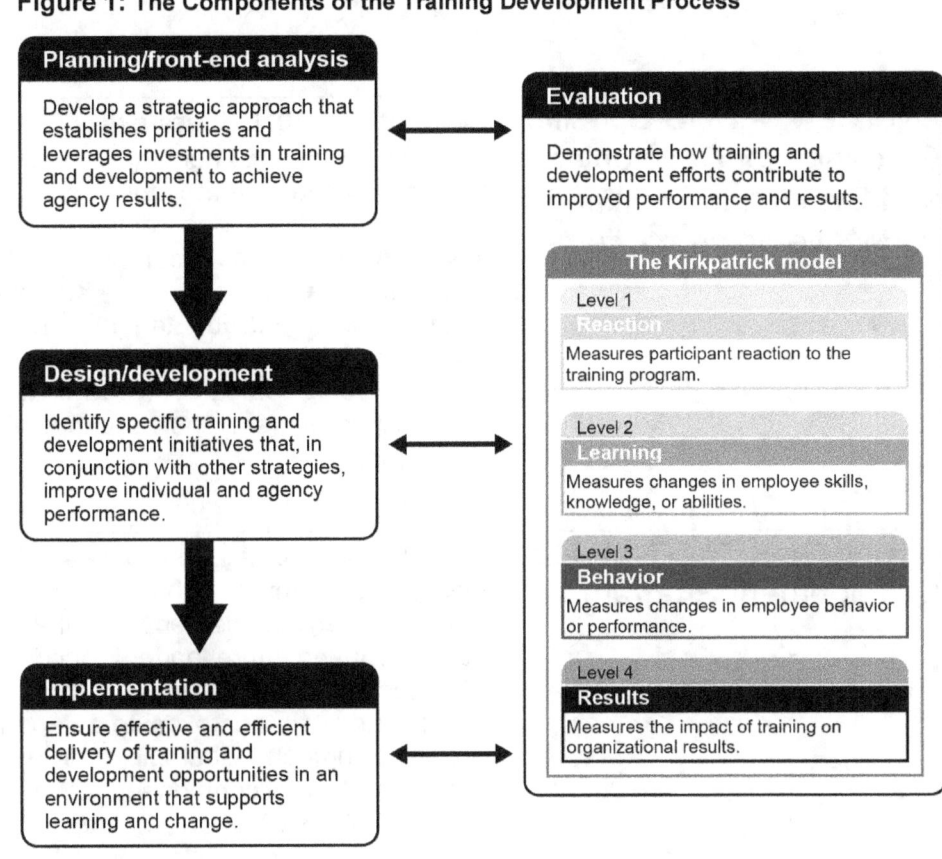

Source: GAO. | GAO-14-688

In addition to utilizing this training development process, agencies may also seek Federal Law Enforcement Training Accreditation (FLETA) for some or all of their training programs and academies. By attaining FLETA accreditation for their training academies or programs, agencies provide assurance that they have voluntarily submitted to a process of self-regulation and have successfully achieved compliance with a set of standards that demonstrate their adherence to quality, effectiveness, and integrity. FLETA accreditation also helps maintain training standards by ensuring that training programs are comprehensively evaluated, using

Kirkpatrick levels 1 through 3 or an equivalent approach, within a 5-year period.[17]

Overview of DHS-Specific Guidance for Developing and Evaluating Training and Development Efforts

In October 2010, DHS issued its *DHS Learning Evaluation Guide*.[18] DHS created the guide to help the department's learning and development community evaluate the effectiveness of training activities in a diverse organization with varied training needs. Among other things, the guidance gives an overview of best practices and provides components with tools they can use to implement the Kirkpatrick model in their training evaluations. In addition, the guide highlights the need for a training evaluation plan to identify and address (1) what is being evaluated, (2) how it is being evaluated, (3) when it is being evaluated, and (4) the factors involving stakeholder expectations, such as agency policies and procedures.

Overview of DHS's Leader Development Program

In 2004, the Secretary of Homeland Security announced the "One DHS" policy, which identified the need for a common leadership competency framework across the department, as well as a unified training curriculum for current and future leaders. Accordingly, DHS established the LDP Office in May 2010 under the Office of the Chief Human Capital Officer to design, develop, and execute a department-wide leadership program that would strengthen leadership at all levels of the DHS workforce. Through the LDP, all DHS components are to invest in developing leaders with skills that transfer across the department, yet retain the agility to balance this with their own mission-focused leader development needs. In January 2011, DHS also developed the Leader Development Framework to serve as a 3- to 5-year strategic roadmap for implementing the LDP. This framework consists of five tiers of leader development programs for employees of different levels, such as the executive and supervisory levels.

In February 2013, DHS issued a directive—Directive 258-02: *Leader Development*—formally establishing responsibilities and policies related to leader development at DHS through the LDP, as well as instructions for implementing the directive. This directive specifies that the LDP is, among

---

[17]FLETA, *FLETA Standards and Procedures* (Glynco, Georgia: 2010).

[18]DHS, *DHS Learning Evaluation Guide.*

other things, to delineate requirements and activities to be implemented by components. The LDP is also to develop and manage centrally coordinated and high-potential programs for developing employees to fill future leader positions.

DHS Processes for Evaluating Training Programs Could Be Better Documented and More Reliably Capture Costs

DHS components have documented processes in place for evaluating their training programs and have used evaluation feedback to improve their training offerings; however, their documented processes varied on the extent to which selected attributes of an effective training evaluation process were included. Further, DHS identified opportunities for efficiencies and cost savings, but varying approaches for capturing training costs across the department affect DHS's ability to reliably capture and track its training costs department-wide.

DHS Components Use Evaluations to Improve Training, but Documenting Selected Attributes of Their Evaluation Processes Could Improve Transparency and Consistency

The five DHS components in our review have a documented process in place for evaluating their training programs using the Kirkpatrick four-level model. However, their documented evaluation processes varied on the extent to which they included selected attributes of an effective evaluation process. Components use the results of their evaluations to make improvements to the training programs and assess training needs. For example, components used evaluation feedback to improve the delivery of training content, such as through additional hands-on training, and the use of e-learning. Table 2 provides such an example for each component.

Table 2: Examples of Department of Homeland Security Components' Use of Evaluation Feedback to Improve Training

Component	Examples of evaluation feedback leading to course improvements
U.S. Customs and Border Protection (CBP)	CBP received consistent feedback from participants in the CBP Officer Basic Training course that they wanted more practical exercises and hands-on training. CBP then revised the program to cover more of the content through practical exercises, rather than classroom instruction.
U.S. Immigration and Customs Enforcement (ICE)	ICE received feedback from participants in its Supervisory Leadership Training program that some of the content of the online and classroom portions of the course was duplicative. As a result, ICE consolidated the content into an online precourse assignment and shortened the course from 2 weeks to 1 week.
Coast Guard	The Basic Boarding Officer course was initially designed for all boarding officers, which included training in the Ports, Waterways Coastal Security (PWCS) mission. Through analysis conducted in 2008, as well as through follow-up evaluation efforts, the Coast Guard determined that a majority of the participants in the course did not perform the PWCS mission. As a result, the Coast Guard extracted the PWCS mission portion of the course from the original Basic Boarding Officer course and made it into a new course.
Transportation Security Administration (TSA)	TSA received feedback from participants in its cultural awareness training program that the content needed to be more specific to the duties of transportation security officers (TSO). As a result, TSA consolidated content from three courses into a single course with more details about identifying cultural and religious norms to differentiate between benign behavior and those that may merit more scrutiny.
Federal Law Enforcement Training Center (FLETC)	In FLETC's Criminal Investigator Training Program (CITP) level 3 evaluations, supervisors and students requested more M4 weapon systems training. Specifically, students wanted to familiarize themselves with M4 weapons before advanced training. After receiving this feedback, FLETC discussed the issue during the Curriculum Review Conference and decided to introduce the M4 weapon system into the CITP.

Source: GAO Interviews with components and GAO assessment of completed evaluations. I GAO-14-688

OPM guidance on training evaluation, DHS's learning evaluation guidance, and our prior work on effective training and development programs identify various attributes for effective training evaluations. Consistent with these criteria, the attributes of an effective training evaluation process include communicating (1) the goals the training programs are supposed to achieve, (2) which training programs will be evaluated, (3) the methodology for conducting the evaluations, (4) timeframes for conducting the evaluation, (5) roles and responsibilities for evaluation efforts, and (6) how the evaluation results will be used.[19]

All DHS components in our review reflected a number of the attributes of an effective training evaluation process in their documentation. For example, all components included information on identifying goals that the training programs are to achieve, identifying which training programs are to be evaluated, and explaining how the evaluation results will be used. Table 3 presents information on the extent to which each component's documented evaluation process includes these attributes, and additional details about component ratings are explained in appendix II.

---

[19]For our analysis, we selected the attributes that were consistently identified in relevant guidance related to training evaluation, such as DHS's *Learning Evaluation Guide*, OPM's *Training Evaluation Field Guide*, and our prior work in *Human Capital: A Guide for Assessing Strategic Training and Development Efforts in the Federal Government* (GAO-04-546G). Specifically, to align with OPM regulations that require agencies to evaluate training effectiveness, in October 2010, DHS issued informal guidance on approaches to evaluating training. This guidance highlights the need for an evaluation plan that includes information on (1) what is being evaluated, (2) how it is being evaluated, (3) when it is being evaluated, and (4) the factors that influence the achievement of stakeholder expectations. In addition, GAO has previously identified key attributes of effective training and development programs, which include establishing a plan that sets priorities for evaluations; systematically covers the methods, timing, and responsibilities for data collection; and explains how the results of the evaluations will be used. See, for example, GAO-04-546G. These attributes also align with those identified in *Standards for Internal Control in the Federal Government*, which call for agencies to document the plans, methods, and procedures used to meet missions, goals, and objectives and support performance-based management practices.

Table 3: Presence of Effective Training Attributes in the Department of Homeland Security's (DHS) Documented Training Evaluation Processes

Component	Establishes goals about what the training program is supposed to achieve	Indicates which programs are being evaluated	Explains methodology used to conduct the evaluation	Presents timeframes for conducting the evaluation	Presents roles and responsibilities for evaluation efforts	Explains how the evaluation results will be used
U.S. Customs and Border Protection (CBP)	●	●	◗	◗	◗	●
U.S. Immigration and Customs Enforcement (ICE)	●	●	●	●	◗	●
Coast Guard	●	●	●	◗	●	●
Transportation Security Administration (TSA)[a]	●	●	◗	◗	◗	●
Federal Law Enforcement Training Center (FLETC)	●	●	◗	●	●	●

●: The component's documented evaluation processes fully included information to meet the attribute for all aspects of their evaluation process.

◗: The component's documented evaluation processes included some information to address a given attribute but did not include information to fully and consistently meet all parts of the attribute. This includes, for example, incomplete evaluation processes or incomplete information to address a given attribute for certain levels of the evaluation.

Source: GAO analysis of documented evaluation processes. I GAO-14-688

[a]The analysis of TSA's documented evaluation process is based on a review of TSA's draft training development standards. These training standards are to be followed by all TSA training programs. For this analysis, we excluded the evaluation processes that are specific to the federal air marshals' training programs alone because they are governed by separate evaluation processes to retain FLETA accreditation that do not apply to other aspects of training at TSA.

However, components varied on the extent to which they included information in their documentation about evaluation methodologies, timeframes, and roles and responsibilities for evaluation. For example,

- Evaluation methodologies: Each component's documentation indicates that its training programs are to be evaluated using the Kirkpatrick model. However, only ICE's and the Coast Guard's documentation specify the methods to be used when performing each Kirkpatrick level of evaluation.

The other three components' documentation does not specify how each Kirkpatrick level of evaluation is to be performed in practice.

- Timeframes: ICE and FLETC's documented evaluation processes fully presents timeframes for evaluations, but documentation for the remaining three components does not. For example, all of the components' documentation identified the timeframes for the initial steps of completing evaluation surveys and collecting data. However, ICE and FLETC's documentation also communicated timeframes for the subsequent steps for analyzing the results of the evaluation.

- Roles and responsibilities: We found that three of five components did not consistently outline the roles and responsibilities for the evaluation efforts. For instance, two components, CBP and ICE, communicate information on roles and responsibilities for some parts of the process, but do not present this information for others. TSA's documentation did not communicate information on the specific roles and responsibilities within the Office of Training and Workforce Engagement (OTWE) for evaluation activities.

Officials at one component, CBP, told us that since training at CBP is more decentralized through separate academies that follow their own processes, their documentation did not include some attributes of effective training and development programs, as their training standards were intended to be more of a "how-to guide" rather than a formal step-by-step methodology. According to TSA officials, they did not fully include certain attributes such as explaining the methodology to be used to conduct the evaluations and defining roles and responsibilities because their process is still under development and agreement on this information has not yet been reached internally. TSA officials stated that their documentation is to be finalized by the first quarter of fiscal year 2015. Officials at the Coast Guard told us that their documentation did not include information on the timeframes for analyzing the results, but they plan to rectify this with their current effort in fiscal year 2014 to revise their evaluation processes.[20] Two of the five components–ICE, and FLETC—

---

[20]The Coast Guard noted that its training evaluation program has been continually improved since the original policy was issued in 1998 by providing clarifications with updates in 2004, 2008, and 2011. While each updated policy provided more clarity regarding the process, some aspects, such as timeframes for analyzing evaluation results, remain undocumented.

did not provide a reason for why their documentation did not include all of the attributes of effective training and development programs.

All DHS components agreed that having a documented training evaluation process provides benefits, such as helping to ensure consistency and transparency across the organization. Accordingly, as previously noted, TSA is working to finalize its training evaluation process. In addition, officials from two components, the Coast Guard and CBP, stated they plan to revise their documented processes in the near future. Specifically, according to Coast Guard officials, revisions to the training evaluation process are being made to more explicitly communicate their process, enhance standardization, and facilitate prioritizing its training evaluation efforts to focus on the most mission-critical training needs. As the process is under way, Coast Guard officials were not able to provide an estimate for when these revisions should be completed. Similarly, according to CBP officials, they plan to review and revise CBP's training evaluation process to ensure consistency across the component. CBP believes this is necessary given that its training functions have become more decentralized since its last training evaluation process came into effect in 2008. According to CBP officials, the target completion of revisions is fiscal year 2015, after the reorganization of CBP's Office of Training and Development is complete.

By ensuring that the components' documented evaluation processes fully address attributes for effective training as they are drafted, updated or revised, DHS would have better assurance that the components have complete information to guide its efforts in conducting effective evaluations. Moreover, such documentation could help ensure that evaluation processes for assessing whether training programs appropriately support component and DHS needs can be repeated and implemented consistently. As components draft, update, and revise their documented evaluation processes, incorporating or more fully addressing the aforementioned attributes of effective training evaluations could help to ensure that components clearly communicate all aspects of their evaluation processes and that employees can consistently implement them.

DHS and Components Have Identified Opportunities for Efficiencies and Cost Savings, but Varying Approaches for Capturing Training Costs at DHS Affect Reliability

All DHS components reported reviewing the merits of different delivery mechanisms (e.g., classroom or computer-based training) to determine which mix would be the most efficient for at least one of their training programs. In addition, four of five components—CBP, the Coast Guard, ICE, and TSA—provided at least one illustrative example of how they used a mix of webinars, online learning, and classroom instructor-led training to develop a blended learning approach that improved cost-effectiveness. For example, in June 2013, TSA implemented webinar training for Sensitive Security Information (SSI), which helped TSA avoid travel costs and led to an estimated $855,026 in cost savings. In addition, ICE developed online training for Fourth Amendment instruction, which helped reduce the course length by 1 week, contributing to opportunity cost savings and savings in room and board totaling about $4.8 million over a 5-year period.[21] The components we reviewed that used webinars or online learning stated that these delivery mechanisms did not adversely affect the quality of training offered in these instances. Furthermore, all DHS components reported that they have evaluated at least one training program to determine how to streamline or consolidate the training to make it more cost-effective. For example, FLETC adopted firearms simulation technology and more cost-effective ammunition, and according to our analysis of FLETC data, led to about $2.2 million in cost savings. See figure 2 for a photographic example of training using firearms simulation.

---

[21]ICE staff forgo productivity in assigned duties while training. This lost productivity, or opportunity cost, is estimated by wages and benefits paid during training. Reducing course length means a lower opportunity cost, thus, opportunity cost savings.

Figure 2: Firearms Simulation Training at FLETC

Source: Federal Law Enforcement Training Center. | GAO-14-688

Similarly, at the department level, OCHCO has taken steps to streamline mandatory department-wide training requirements for counterintelligence and records management training. For example, based on review of legal requirements, OCHCO found that it could streamline mandatory records management training by consolidating multiple annual training requirements into a single course. According to OCHCO officials and our analysis of OCHCO data, this effort could lead to a potential cost saving of about $57.1 million over a 5-year period.[22]

Table 4 provides illustrative examples of actions OCHCO and selected components have taken to improve the cost-effectiveness of training and the estimated cost savings from these actions over a 5-year period, according to our analysis of OCHCO and DHS components.

---

[22]According to OCHCO officials, leveraging existing resources, collaboration and sharing in leadership development programs reportedly helped DHS components save expenses.

Table 4: Five-Year Estimates of Cost Savings from Improved Efficiencies in Training and Development Programs by OCHCO and Selected Department of Homeland Security (DHS) Components

DHS and selected components	Training program	General description	Reported cost savings
DHS's Office of the Chief Human Capital Officer (OCHCO)	Mandatory training	Consolidation of mandatory training into a single course and limiting training to employees who are required by law to complete the training	According to our analysis of OCHCO data, there is about $57.1 million in opportunity cost savings (beginning in fiscal year 2013).
U.S. Customs and Border Protection (CBP)	Supervisory leadership training	Consolidation of supervisory leadership training, including webinar training, and sharing of training programs with field offices	CBP avoided travel costs and reported about $4.9 million in cost savings (beginning in fiscal year 2012).
U.S. Immigration and Customs Enforcement (ICE)	Field Operations Training Program	Development of a virtual university course to deliver online learning for Fourth Amendment training.	According to our analysis of ICE data, there is about $4.8 million in budget and opportunity cost savings (beginning in fiscal year 2011).
Federal Law Enforcement Training Center (FLETC)	Firearms training	Use of cost-effective ammunition and simulation technology for firearms training	According to our analysis of FLETC data, there is about $2.2 million in cost savings associated with using more cost-effective ammunition and a simulated firearms training program (beginning in fiscal year 2013).
U.S. Coast Guard	Aircraft training	Use of simulated technology for flight training	The Coast Guard reported that it reduced flight hours for aviation training, which, according to our analysis of Coast Guard data, led to an estimated $7.3 million in cost savings (beginning in fiscal year 2014).
Transportation Security Administration (TSA)	Risk-Based Security training	Shortening the length of training	TSA shortened the length of training from 8 hours to 4 hours, which, according to our analysis of TSA data, led to an estimated $18.6 million in opportunity cost savings (beginning in fiscal year 2013).[a]

Source: GAO analysis of DHS information. I GAO-14-688

[a]TSA staff forgo productivity in assigned duties while training. This lost productivity, or opportunity cost, is estimated by wages and benefits paid during training. Reducing course length means a lower opportunity cost, thus opportunity cost savings.

Starting in fiscal year 2014, CBP adopted a new approach to improve the identification of efficiencies in training, including regular reviews of training justification, cost, and prioritization of training needs. Though the process is not yet documented in policy, directives, or standard operating procedures, CBP officials report that it has allowed them to identify training cost discrepancies more consistently and efficiently. For example, according to CBP officials, their approach includes tracking key cost elements, such as travel, lodging, meal, rental vehicle requirements; duration of training; instructor costs; and contract costs, for all training courses under separate codes. Further, according to these officials, this allows CBP to better compare costs for course execution, such as the cost of course resources (e.g., delivery location, equipment, etc.) and related travel, if any, from year to year. In addition, CBP uses these data to challenge requests for training and identify possible alternatives for delivering existing courses at a reduced cost. The process also provides CBP with a vehicle for better projecting training costs. According to CBP officials, the new approach created requirements that internal offices provide more precise estimates of the number of participants attending training, which reportedly helped CBP more efficiently allocate about $5.8 million in fiscal year 2013. Before the new process was implemented, internal offices could not commit to filling training courses and slots, resulting in CBP's Office of Training and Development overprojecting about $7 million in training costs in fiscal year 2012, which was returned to CBP. According to CBP officials, leadership change, overestimation of training funding needs, and spending reductions under sequestration in fiscal year 2013 were some of the key reasons for adopting this new approach.[23] CBP officials reported that by refining cost projections, CBP improved their ability to approve more training within allocated budgetary resources.[24] For example, based on the new approach in fiscal year 2014, CBP identified surplus training funds from unfilled training slots and class cancellations early enough to enhance training programs.

In addition, although DHS and components provided illustrative examples of efficiencies in training and cost savings, DHS uses different methods to capture training costs. DHS, through OCHCO, has worked to capture the cost and delivery of DHS's training and development programs. However, at DHS headquarters and at the component level, there are inconsistencies in how training costs are captured across the department that have made it a challenge to accurately and reliably capture these

---

[23]On March 1, 2013, pursuant to the Balanced Budget and Emergency Deficit Control Act of 1985, as amended, the President ordered an across-the-board cancellation of budgetary resources—known as sequestration—to achieve $85.3 billion in reductions across federal government accounts. See 2 U.S.C. § 901a. The financial impact of sequestration on DHS was about $2.4 billion. GAO has previously reported on the impact of sequestration. See, for example, GAO, *2013 Sequestration: Agencies Reduced Some Services and Investments, while Taking Certain Actions to Mitigate Effects,* GAO-14-244 (Washington, D.C.: Mar. 6, 2014) and *2013 Sequestration: Selected Agencies Reduced Some Services and Investments, While Taking Short-Term Actions to Mitigate Effects,* GAO-14-452 (Washington, D.C.: May 28, 2014).

[24]CBP's Office of Training and Development has visibility for training programs under the National Training Plan. For any courses outside the National Training Plan, CBP has to perform a data call to understand what training is being delivered and what the costs are at each of the program offices.

GAO-14-688 DHS Training

costs across DHS. For example, OCHCO officials explained that the lack of a centralized funding source and disparate financial management systems used by components created challenges in reliably capturing training costs. Components also often capture training costs differently from one another, which can contribute to inconsistencies among training costs captured at DHS. Training costs may, for example, include expenses for instructional development, participant and instructor salary and benefits, equipment costs, and travel and per diem expenses. Accordingly, OCHCO officials report that some components include conferences as a training cost while others do not, and some components did not include mission-critical law enforcement training costs when they provided department-wide training costs.[25]

In fiscal year 2012, the DHS Undersecretary for Management requested that OCHCO collect training cost data from components. During this process, OCHCO relied on senior-level data requests to retrieve annual training expenditure information from components. According to OCHCO officials, the senior-level data call process revealed that training cost data had limited reliability because some components were not consistent in determining the types of mission-critical training costs they provided, among other things.[26] Given ongoing concerns about data reliability, OCHCO officials noted that it would be difficult to update and reliably aggregate department-wide training costs for fiscal year 2013.[27] According to OCHCO officials, given budget constraints, it is difficult for OCHCO to make good investment decisions about training when they do not know how components spend their training dollars.

---

[25]During the recent senior-level data call for department-wide training costs in fiscal year 2012, OCHCO officials stated that one DHS component did not include law enforcement training costs.

[26]We also previously reported that DHS faced challenges implementing a mechanism to assess management and administration activities, partly because DHS components defined spending differently. GAO, *DHS Management and Administration Spending: Reliable Data Could Help DHS Better Estimate Resource Requests,* GAO-14-27 (Washington, D.C.: Dec. 4, 2013).

[27]According to OCHCO officials, the DHS Undersecretary of Management had to request annual training costs department-wide for fiscal year 2012. Without a senior-level data request and given the reliability concerns with training data, OCHCO is unlikely to update and aggregate training costs for fiscal year 2013.

In addition, according to discussions with ICE officials, we found that the cost of ICE's training and development programs may not be consistently and accurately captured. For example, ICE officials stated that participant and instructor salaries are consistently tracked as part of training costs, but travel expenses are less consistently tracked for all ICE internal training programs. Further, according to ICE officials, incomplete definitions of training and inconsistency in how costs are tracked also contribute to shortfalls in reliably capturing training costs. ICE officials reported, for example, that they cannot reliably capture training costs from one of ICE's internal departments and, instead, need to rely on sporadic data calls to retrieve training budget and expenditure information from its departments. ICE officials reported concerns about the reliability of this process, partly because of concerns about inconsistent coding schemes for tracking similar training activities and the lack of third-party checks on the reliability of how training information is coded. As of August 2014, ICE officials report that their Office of the Chief Financial Officer is working to standardize its coding schemes—or object class reporting—across ICE programs and plans to implement the revised coding standards in fiscal year 2015.

OCHCO and ICE officials we met with acknowledged that the department has not identified all challenges that prevent DHS from accurately capturing training costs department-wide, but they have taken some preliminary steps toward more consistently defining training and capturing costs. For example, while DHS has not issued central guidance on what should be included in training costs, OCHCO officials noted that they provided a glossary of terms to components in December 2007 to help establish an initial definition of training department-wide. Although the glossary clarifies a number of training-related terms, it does not provide requirements for tracking training costs consistently across components. For example, the glossary notes that training program costs are calculated differently on a component basis. Further, according to ICE and OCHCO officials, DHS discussed the issue of accurately and reliably capturing training and development costs across the department as part of its Training Leaders Council in May 2014. OCHCO officials reported that the use of a standard form for requesting training, known as the federal government's Standard Form 182, *Authorization, Agreement, and Certification of Training*, may be one method for improving the tracking of training costs. For example, the Form 182 may help provide for consistent definitions and methods for capturing certain training costs. However, while use of the standard Form 182 would be a positive step, it may not address certain reliability concerns associated with capturing training costs at DHS. For example, the approach may not prevent the duplicative capturing of procurement-related training costs or shortfalls in how training information is entered and captured in each component's systems. According to the DHS Chief Learning Officer, requiring the use of the Form 182 DHS-wide is still in the preliminary stages of consideration and would require accompanying policy changes. As DHS has not yet made a decision on whether to require use of the Form 182, it does not yet have timeframes for implementing this proposal.

One leading training investment practice is that agencies should capture the cost and delivery of their training and development programs.[28] Our prior work has also shown that agencies need reliable information on how much they spend on training and for what purposes.[29] To capture the cost and delivery of training and development programs, agencies need credible and reliable data from learning management systems as well as accounting, financial, and performance reporting systems. To the extent possible, agencies also need to ensure data consistency across the organization (such as having data elements that are pulled from various systems representing the same type of information). Variations in the methods used to collect data can greatly affect the analysis of uniform, high-quality data on the cost and delivery of training and development programs. Given today's budgetary constraints and the need to effectively utilize and account for all federal dollars, identifying existing challenges that prevent DHS from accurately capturing training costs department-wide and, to the extent that the benefits exceed the costs, implementing corrective measures to overcome these challenges, could enhance DHS's resource stewardship.

---

[28]GAO, *Federal Training Investments: Office of Personnel Management and Agencies Can Do More to Ensure Cost-Effective Decisions*, GAO-12-878 (Washington, D.C.: September 2012). As part of this work, GAO identified leading practices in federal training investments. GAO identified these practices based on a review of prior GAO studies; expert studies by the Corporate Leadership Council and statutory, regulatory and executive order training requirements. See GAO-12-878 for additional details on the methodology used.

[29]GAO-04-546G. As part of this work, GAO identified key principles and key questions federal agencies can use to ensure that their training and development investments are targeted strategically. GAO identified these principles and key questions through consultations with government officials and experts in the private sector, academia, and nonprofit organizations; examinations of laws and regulations related to training and development in the federal government; and reviewing the sizeable body of literature on training and development issues, including previous GAO products on a range of human capital topics. See GAO-04-546G for additional details on the methodology used.

DHS Is Implementing a Department-wide Leader Development Framework, but Could Strengthen Its Program Assessment

DHS's Leader Development Program Office is in the process of implementing a department-wide, five-tier Leader Development Framework to build leadership skills across all staff levels. While DHS components generally stated that the LDP framework is beneficial, they raised concerns about its training requirements, which the LDP Office's planned evaluation efforts may address. Further, the LDP office has developed a program-wide assessment approach to analyze the impact of the LDP that includes tracking 12 performance measures over time. However, the LDP Office could strengthen its performance measurement efforts by clearly identifying its program goals and better incorporating key attributes of successful performance measures we have previously identified.

DHS Has Implemented Portions of the Department-wide Leader Development Framework, and Components Deliver Additional Programs to Develop Their Leaders

DHS has implemented programs in support of two of five tiers within its department-wide Leader Development Framework, and the selected components in our review also deliver additional leader development programs for supervisors, managers, and executives. As previously discussed, DHS established the LDP Office in May 2010 to design, develop, and execute a department-wide program to strengthen leadership at all levels of the DHS workforce. In January 2011, DHS approved the Leader Development Framework as a 3- to 5-year strategic roadmap for implementing the LDP. This Leader Development Framework consists of five tiers that identify envisioned leader development programs for employees of different levels. These tiers, and the employees they include, are the following:

- executive (members of the Senior Executive Service, Coast Guard admirals, and selected other leaders),
- manager (nonexecutive employees who supervise other supervisors, lead through subordinate supervisors, and formally supervise at least one supervisory employee),
- supervisor (employees who accomplish work through, and are directly responsible for, the work of nonsupervisory employees, and who formally supervise only nonsupervisory employees),
- team lead (nonsupervisory employees formally designated as such or tasked to guide a group of people to results on a program, project, initiative, or task force), and
- team member (nonsupervisory DHS employees).

The LDP Office has implemented programs within two of the five Leader Development Framework tiers (supervisor and executive), initiated program development within two tiers (team lead and team member), and plans to begin program development within one tier during fiscal year

2014 (manager). According to the LDP Manager, the office prioritized implementation of the supervisor tier at the direction of the then deputy secretary, who identified supervisors as a critical nexus between strategic leadership and employee performance. The LDP Manager stated that the office also prioritized implementation of the executive tier because OCHCO officials were familiar with best practices for instruction for new executives and the then deputy secretary identified particular value in providing new executives with consistent instruction. Within the supervisor tier, the LDP Office has established the Cornerstone Program, which consists of a set of baseline requirements for new and seasoned supervisors at all levels.[30] DHS components may fulfill Cornerstone Program requirements through new or existing training programs, cross-component programming, or a combination thereof. Within the executive tier, the LDP Office centrally administers the 3-week Capstone Cohort Program, which includes discussion forums, operational site visits, and learning activities intended to address real-world strategic issues. As the program is currently implemented, whereas components may elect to send participants to the Capstone Program, they are required by DHS to implement Cornerstone Program requirements.[31]

In addition to implementing programs to support the supervisor and executive leader development framework tiers, the LDP Office has assumed responsibility for administering two preexisting DHS programs, the Senior Executive Service Candidate Development Program and DHS Fellows. These programs are not a part of any one tier, as their intended participants may span framework tiers.[32] For example, the Senior

---

[30]Cornerstone Program requirements were developed in support of the supervisor tier. However, they apply to all first-time supervisors, individuals who are new to supervising within the federal government, and seasoned and experienced federal supervisors, even if the individuals' positions meet the definitions of managers or executives.

[31]According to OCHCO officials, OCHCO has used funding from the Undersecretary for Management Salaries and Expenses account to fund Capstone, but the program has not been institutionalized in the department's budget. If the Capstone Program receives sustained funding in the future, LDP officials stated that DHS may begin to require new executives to participate in the program.

[32]According to the LDP Manager, the LDP Office has significantly revised the selection processes and curricula for these programs since assuming responsibility for them. For example, the LDP Manager stated that the LDP Office instituted a new process for assessing Senior Executive Service Candidate Development Program applications and revised the program's curriculum to, among other things, increase cohort-based, peer-to-peer learning and tailor learning more specifically to the needs of participants and their respective components.

Executive Service Candidate Development Program is designed for Senior Executive Service candidates who aspire to transition into the executive tier. Figure 3, an interactive graphic, describes the development and implementation status of the programs that support each tier as of August 2014. See appendix III for a print version of this figure. LDP Office officials anticipate fully implementing all five tiers of the Leader Development Framework before the end of fiscal year 2016.

Figure 3: Leader Development Framework—Programs and Status, as of August 2014

Move mouse over the program names for more information. For a text version please see app. III.

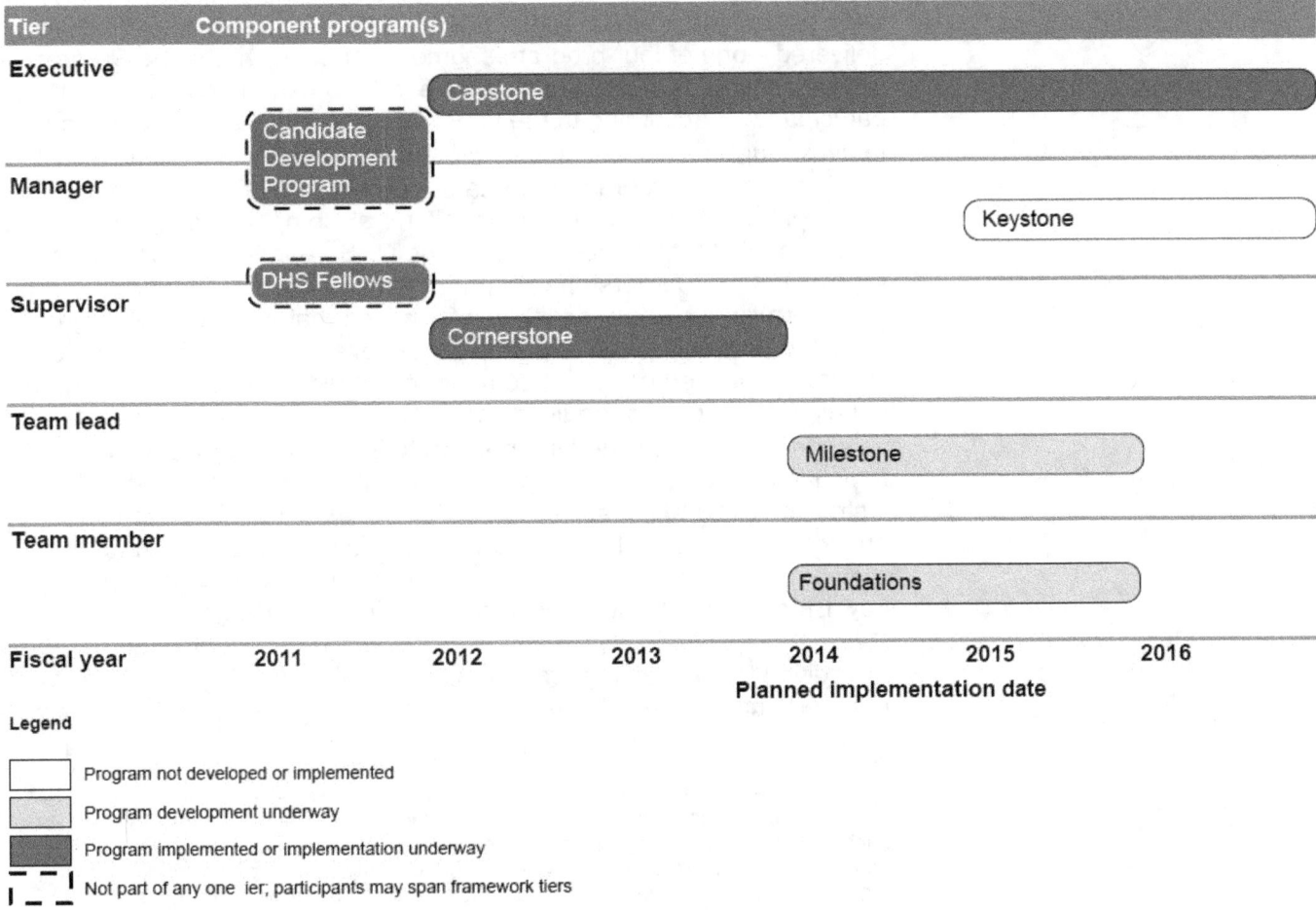

Tier	Component program(s)					
Executive			Capstone			
Manager	Candidate Development Program				Keystone	
Supervisor	DHS Fellows	Cornerstone				
Team lead				Milestone		
Team member				Foundations		
Fiscal year	2011	2012	2013	2014	2015	2016

Planned implementation date

Legend

☐ Program not developed or implemented

▨ Program development underway

▩ Program implemented or implementation underway

⌐ ¬ Not part of any one tier; participants may span framework tiers
└ ┘

Source: GAO analysis of DHS information. | GAO-14-688

The five DHS components selected for our review have all participated in the LDP department-wide programs. In particular, according to LDP Office and component data and officials, all five components have programs in place, as required by DHS, intended to meet the Cornerstone Program requirements. For instance, data from the selected components demonstrate that the Fundamentals of DHS Leadership courses they delivered—one of four program segments of the Cornerstone Program—from fiscal year 2012 through fiscal year 2013 had more than 3,600 participants.[33] According to the LDP Manager, the LDP Office has sought to avoid duplication of effort and costs in components' implementation of the Cornerstone Program. For example, the LDP Office coordinated the development of instructional materials for all components to use to meet requirements for the Understanding the DHS Leadership Commitment segment of the Cornerstone Program, which is for individuals considering the supervisory path. In addition, information that a DHS working group collected from components during initial development of the Cornerstone Program indicated that most components could utilize existing programs to help meet program requirements.[34] Specifically, six of the seven components that provided information to the working group indicated that they had an existing training program that they could use to provide instruction to first-time supervisors. For instance, FLETC uses two preexisting programs to meet Fundamentals of DHS Leadership requirements—the FLETC New Supervisor Training Program and the Law Enforcement Supervisor Leadership Training Program.

In addition to maintaining programs to meet Cornerstone Program requirements, each of the selected components has elected to participate

---

[33]As described in fig. 3, the Cornerstone Program consists of four segments. Data for each of these program segments are maintained separately, but can include overlapping participants, as individuals may have participated in more than one component of the program within a fiscal year. To avoid double-counting program participants, the "3,600 participants" value represents the number of individuals reported to have completed the Fundamentals of DHS Leadership segment of the Cornerstone Program, which is to provide the longest segment of instruction.

[34]In April 2011 a DHS cross-component working group—the DHS Supervisor Working Group—developed proposed requirements for the Cornerstone Program. In order to develop this proposal, the working group collected information from seven DHS components on the extent to which they already had programs in place that met potential requirements, among other things. These components were FLETC, ICE, TSA, CBP, the U.S. Secret Service, the Federal Emergency Management Agency, and DHS headquarters. According to the LDP Manager, the LDP Office built upon this proposal in developing final Cornerstone Program requirements.

in the three department-wide programs administered centrally by the LDP Office—the Capstone Cohort Program, Senior Executive Service Candidate Development Program, and DHS Fellows. In particular, these programs had a total of approximately 60 participants from the selected components from fiscal year 2012 through fiscal year 2013, according to LDP Office data. Table 5 summarizes approximate participation in Leader Development Framework programs that were provided by the selected components to meet department-wide requirements or centrally administered by the LDP from fiscal year 2012 through fiscal year 2013, according to LDP Office and component data.

Table 5: Participation in Department of Homeland Security (DHS) Leader Development Framework Programs Provided by Selected Components or Through the Leader Development Program, Fiscal Years 2012-2013

	Approximate number of participants			
Component	Cornerstone Fundamentals of DHS Leadership[a]	Capstone Cohort Program	Candidate Development Program	DHS Fellows Program
U.S. Customs and Border Protection	1,080	4	8	7
U.S. Immigration and Customs Enforcement	680	2	4	2
Federal Law Enforcement Training Center (FLETC)	20[b]	1	5	1
U.S. Coast Guard	330[c]	2	1	5
Transportation Security Administration	1,505	4	12	4
Total	**3,615**	**13**	**30**	**19**

Source: GAO analysis of DHS information. I GAO-14-688

Notes: Data presented in this table reflect the approximate number of participants in each program. The same individual may have participated in multiple programs.

[a]As described in fig. 3, the Cornerstone Program consists of four segments. Data for each of these program segments are maintained separately, but can include overlapping participants, as individuals may have participated in more than one component of the program within a fiscal year. To avoid double-counting program participants, data presented in this column represent the number of individuals reported to have completed the Fundamentals of DHS Leadership segment of the Cornerstone Program, which is to provide the longest segment of instruction. As DHS tracks data for Cornerstone by completions rather than participants, these data may not include some participants who began, but did not finish, the requirements in a single reporting period.

[b]This value reflects the approximate number of FLETC staff participants. Approximately 340 additional non-FLETC staff from DHS components and participating organizations also completed training FLETC uses to fulfill Cornerstone Fundamentals of DHS Leadership requirements.

[c]Fundamentals of DHS Leadership requires a total of at least 40 hours of development, of which 24 hours are in-person classroom training. The Coast Guard provided students with 40 hours of online instruction, but did not provide students with in-person classroom training because of government sequestration. According to Coast Guard officials, the Coast Guard plans to provide students with 32 hours of classroom training in addition to 40 hours of online instruction beginning in fiscal year 2014.

In addition to the programs administered under the Leader Development Framework, the components in our review also deliver various additional leader development programs. For example, Coast Guard delivers a 1-week course for newly selected executives focused on change management issues and TSA delivers a program for supervisors over a period of 18 to 24 months that includes training, shadowing, mentoring, and other developmental leadership opportunities. Table 6 provides examples of leader development programs delivered by these components at the executive, supervisor, and manager levels.

Table 6: Examples of Leader Development Programs Delivered by Selected Department of Homeland Security (DHS) Components Independent of Department-wide Programming, Fiscal Years 2012-2013

Component	Program name	Description	Intended participant
U.S. Customs and Border Protection (CBP)	Second Level Command Preparation	Six weeks of remote and classroom-based instruction followed by mentoring and project-based learning focused on leadership challenges faced by new CBP managers. This program stresses leadership, ethical decision making, and strategic thinking skills.	Manager
U.S. Immigration and Customs Enforcement (ICE)	Advanced Supervisor Leadership Training	One week of instruction focusing on a supervisor's ability to motivate employees, match strengths and talents to performance, and create an ICE culture of learning.[a]	Manager
Federal Law Enforcement Training Center	Situational Leadership II for Law Enforcement Training Program	Three days of classroom-based instruction intended to provide participants with leadership tools to enhance their effectiveness and success as supervisors. This program teaches participants a specific leadership model to use to develop their subordinates.	Supervisor or manager
U.S. Coast Guard	Executive Change Leadership Program	One-week course for newly selected executives that focuses on issues of personal change management and leading organizational change and performance.	Executive
Transportation Security Administration	Mid-Level Development Program	Over a period of 18 to 24 months, this program aims to prepare participants for critical leadership positions through training, shadowing, mentoring, and other developmental leadership opportunities. The program's focus is to build adequate future leadership capable of replacing leaders who retire or leave and retain experienced personnel with strong, demonstrated leadership skills.	Supervisor

Source: GAO analysis of DHS information. I GAO-14-688

[a]ICE suspended the Advanced Supervisor Leadership Training program in August 2012 because of government sequestration. According to a senior ICE official, as of June 2014, ICE is developing an online version of the program.

As shown in table 7, according to data provided by the selected components, leader development programs they delivered for supervisors, managers, and executives, independent of department-wide programming, from fiscal year 2012 through fiscal year 2013 had a total of more than 10,000 participants.

Table 7: Participation in Leader Development Programs Delivered by Selected Department of Homeland Security Components Independent of Department-wide Programming, Fiscal Years 2012-2013

Component	Approximate participants
U.S. Customs and Border Protection	900
U.S. Immigration and Customs Enforcement	250
Federal Law Enforcement Training Center	360
U.S. Coast Guard	8,630
Transportation Security Administration	160
Total	**10,300**

Source: GAO analysis of DHS information. I GAO-14-688

Note: Data presented in this table reflect the approximate number of participants in the programs provided by each component. The same individual may have participated in multiple programs. In addition, these data do not include participants in computer-based leader development courses that components may purchase from vendors.

Officials from the components in our review generally stated that it is beneficial for their components to provide leader development programs in addition to the LDP department-wide training because, whereas LDP training focuses on more general leadership skills and competencies, component-level training is tailored to the components' unique missions. For example, TSA officials explained that TSA leader development programs focus on developing individuals for TSA's mission-critical occupational areas (e.g., federal security directors and federal air marshals), which require proficiency in a set of leadership and technical competencies unique to TSA. In addition, TSA leader development programs utilize examples that are readily applicable to day-to-day TSA operations, according to these officials. Similarly, according to Coast Guard officials, their leader development programs afford the Coast Guard the opportunity to provide instruction using case studies and in-class discussions on how to lead a Coast Guard workforce in a Coast Guard context.

Component Officials Generally Stated the LDP Framework Is Beneficial, but Raised Concerns about LDP Requirements, Which LDP Assessment Efforts May Address

Component officials we spoke with generally agreed that the LDP is helpful in providing a common framework for leader development training. However, officials from three of the five components we met with raised concerns about the applicability or clarity of certain learning objectives the LDP requires they teach when implementing the Cornerstone Program.[35]

Officials from one component stated that the LDP has established policy and procedures, which help to ensure all components are informed and have consistent definitions and policies related to leader development. Components also identified other benefits of the LDP, such as bringing focus across the department to leader development, allowing for collaboration on leader development activities, and having experienced staff who work solely on leader development issues and programs.

As previously discussed, the Cornerstone Program consists of requirements in four segments, one of which is a course on the fundamentals of DHS leadership that is required for all first-time federal supervisors. In order to fulfill LDP requirements for this course, all components must provide instruction on more than 200 learning objectives that identify content the course must cover.[36] For example, these learning objectives include encouraging respect for individual differences and determining appropriate tasks to delegate. According to DHS guidance on the LDP, all DHS components are to develop leaders with skills that transfer across DHS, yet retain the agility to advance their own unique mission-focused leader development needs. However, officials from two components raised concerns about the applicability of certain objectives that the LDP requires them to teach. For example, officials from one component stated that the learning objective involving supervising a workforce of federal employees and contractors is not universally applicable because supervisors in their component do not supervise contractors. Officials from another component stated that one

---

[35]Of the officials from the three components that raised concerns, officials from one component raised concerns about the applicability of certain learning objectives, officials from another component raised concerns about the clarity of certain learning objectives, and officials from a third component raised concerns about both the applicability and clarity of certain learning objectives. Accordingly, officials from a total of three components raised concerns about the applicability or clarity of certain Fundamentals of DHS Leadership learning objectives.

[36]DHS defines an objective as a specifically defined ability or outcome gained as a result of a planned activity. Department of Homeland Security, *Department of Homeland Security Training Glossary*, Version 1.2 (Washington, D.C.: December 2007).

objective related to supervisors' knowledge of the hiring process does not pertain to new supervisors within their component. According to these component officials, requiring them to teach objectives that are not pertinent to tasks supervisors must perform takes away from instructional time that they could use to teach more relevant content. According to the LDP Manager, the LDP Office established learning objectives in order to meet DHS's direction to ensure sufficient consistency in leader development investment across components, but components may adapt the objectives, as appropriate. For example, TSA requested a waiver from teaching learning objectives focused on Title 5 of the U.S. Code, from which TSA is generally exempt.[37] The LDP Manager granted the waiver, and suggested that TSA replace instruction focused on Title 5 with instruction on related subjects applicable to TSA. However, officials from the two components that raised concerns were not aware that Cornerstone Program requirements provided them with this flexibility.[38]

Officials from two components raised concerns that some of the learning objectives required to be taught under the Fundamentals of DHS Leadership course do not clearly articulate what the training must cover, and that they are not written with standards that can be measured or observed. For example, according to officials from one component, some Fundamentals of DHS Leadership objectives are not consistent with their component's standards, which require that performance objectives include condition, measurable performance behavior, and a standard that specifies the degree of quality expected in performance. For instance, one of the learning objectives that officials identified as not meeting these requirements states, "Recognize a recent study that reported 48 percent of workers surveyed responded to job pressure by performing illegal or unethical activities; 58 percent considered acting illegally or unethically." A senior official from this component explained that this can result in implementation and evaluation challenges—if it is unclear what the

---

[37]49 U.S.C. § 114(n).

[38]The LDP Office has undertaken efforts to evaluate component compliance with Cornerstone Program requirements. Specifically, in December 2011 the LDP Office facilitated an audit to evaluate component compliance with the Fundamentals of DHS Leadership requirements, including the learning objectives that components are to teach. Components were encouraged to use the findings of this audit to guide course modifications that would better support the required Fundamentals of DHS Leadership learning objectives. The LDP Office contracted a subsequent review that was completed in December 2013 to evaluate component progress aligning their curricula with the Fundamentals of DHS Leadership requirements.

outcome of an objective is supposed to be, it is difficult to know how to implement it or evaluate its implementation. This official also stated that officials from his component voiced their concerns about the clarity of learning objectives to DHS headquarters, but DHS did not change them. According to LDP Office officials, they solicited input from components on Cornerstone Program requirements and adopted selected changes. In particular, according to the LDP Manager, the LDP Office solicited input from components during four informal and two formal reviews of Cornerstone Program requirements.[39]

The LDP Office has also awarded a contract for an assessment beginning in February 2014 that includes evaluation of the Fundamentals of DHS Leadership's learning objectives. Scheduled for completion by September 2014, this assessment may help to address concerns raised by components. This assessment is to determine the Cornerstone Program's overall implementation status, determine the effectiveness of the program's products and elements, evaluate the efficacy of the Fundamentals of DHS Leadership's learning objectives, and recommend specific tactical and strategic changes for improving program effectiveness.

Clearly Identifying Program Goals and Enhancing Performance Measures Could Strengthen LDP Assessment Efforts

The LDP has developed a program-wide assessment approach intended to analyze the impact of the LDP over time and assess whether the program is targeting the right things in the right way. However, the LDP Office could strengthen this assessment approach by more clearly identifying its program goals and ensuring its 12 performance measures incorporate key attributes of successful performance measures we have previously identified.[40] The LDP's assessment approach applies to all LDP program elements, including Capstone, Cornerstone, and other programs. The approach consists of (1) biannually collecting and analyzing completion rate data for all LDP programs implemented by components, (2) collecting and analyzing responses to six core evaluation questions immediately following each developmental activity and 6

---

[39]According to LDP officials, the informal reviews included discussing proposed Cornerstone Program requirements with component representatives during meetings or by e-mail and soliciting their written feedback. The formal reviews included executive-level review and certification of Cornerstone Program requirements.

[40]GAO-03-143.

months later, and (3) tracking 12 program performance measures. Table 8 provides some examples of these 12 measures.

Table 8: Examples of Department of Homeland Security (DHS) Leader Development Program (LDP) Performance Measures

- Immediate participant feedback rating on core evaluation question "I would recommend this developmental activity to a colleague at my leader level"
- Number of participants in "Understanding the DHS Leadership Commitment" online or in-person offerings
- Percentage of developmental activities that fulfill LDP requirements delivered with shared resources
- Overall "Best Places to Work" in the federal government ranking[a]

Source: GAO analysis of DHS information. I GAO-14-688

[a]The Best Places to Work ranking is published by the Partnership for Public Service and is derived from results of the Office of Personnel Management's Federal Employee Viewpoint Survey (FEVS)—a tool that measures employees' perceptions of whether and to what extent conditions characterizing successful organizations are present in their agency. In particular, according to the Partnership for Public Service, the Best Places to Work ranking is based on employee responses to three FEVS assessment items: (1) I recommend my organization as a good place to work. (2) Considering everything, how satisfied are you with your job? (3) Considering everything, how satisfied are you with your organization?

For more detailed information about the LDP's assessment approach, see appendix IV.

Developing this assessment approach is a positive step toward assessing the effectiveness of the LDP. However, the LDP Office has not clearly identified goals for the program, and the 12 measures that the office has developed to assess its performance do not consistently exhibit attributes we have previously identified as key for successful measurement. These key attributes include having linkage with division- and agency-wide goals, being clear, and having measurable targets.[41] Table 9 presents definitions of these attributes along with potentially adverse consequences of not meeting them.

---

[41]GAO-03-143. See app. I for a more complete description of our methodology, including how we selected these three key attributes against which to assess LDP's measures.

Table 9: Selected Key Attributes of Successful Performance Measures

Attribute	Definition	Potential adverse consequences of not meeting attribute
Linkage	Measure aligns with division- and agency-wide goals and mission and is clearly communicated throughout the organization.	Behaviors and incentives created by measures do not support achieving division- or agency-wide goals or mission.
Clarity	Measure is clearly stated and the name and definition are consistent with the methodology used to calculate it.	Data could be confusing and misleading to users.
Measurable target	Measure has a numerical goal.	Cannot tell whether performance is meeting expectations.

Source: GAO. I GAO-14-688

Performance measurement is the ongoing monitoring and reporting of program accomplishments, particularly progress toward preestablished goals. We have previously reported that performance measurement allows organizations to track progress in achieving their goals and gives managers crucial information to identify gaps in program performance and plan any needed improvements.[42] In addition, according to *Standards for Internal Control in the Federal Government*, managers need to compare actual performance against planned or expected results and analyze significant differences.[43] We observed the following when assessing the LDP's performance measures against these selected key attributes:

- Linkage: The LDP's 12 performance measures do not clearly link with program goals and linkage is not clearly communicated throughout the organization. The LDP has identified working program goals, but they are disparately documented and not clearly identified as goals. When we asked LDP Office officials to identify the LDP's goals, the LDP Manager

---

[42] GAO, *Executive Guide: Effectively Implementing the Government Performance and Results Act*, GAO/GGD-96-118 (Washington, D.C.: June 1996). While the Government Performance and Results Act is applicable to the department or agency level, performance goals and measures are important management tools applicable to all levels of an agency, including the program, project, or activity level, consistent with leading management practices and internal controls related to performance monitoring.

[43] GAO/AIMD-00-21.3.1.

referred us to statements in Directive 258-02: *Leader Development*, and provided us with a list of working program goals assembled from statements in various LDP materials. These working program goals included, for example, using best practices to maximize effectiveness and elevating the importance of developing leaders department-wide. However, neither the directive nor LDP materials clearly identify or refer to the statements the manager directed us to as goals. Given that the LDP's identified working program goals are disparately documented and not clearly identified as goals, it is unclear whether the LDP's 12 performance measures align with the statements and working program goals the LDP Manager identified. We tried to identify linkage between the LDP's 12 performance measures and the informal goals the LDP Manager identified, but could not determine definitively how they relate.

According to the LDP Manager, the LDP Office did not clearly document the program's goals in one place or record their linkage to the program's performance measures because it established the goals as it developed programs to support the Leader Development Framework. In addition, the LDP Manager stated that DHS's strategic human capital–related plans—which include goals—were under development when the office developed the measures. The LDP Manager explained that, in developing the performance measures, an LDP program official used DHS department-wide strategic plans, direction from DHS officials and stakeholders, and guidance from the *DHS Learning Evaluation Guide*—which provides guidance for evaluating the effectiveness of training activities—to determine categories for the performance measures and then developed measures pertaining to each category.[44] In addition, DHS uses data that the LDP Office collects for its performance measures for strategic planning and reporting, according to the LDP Manager. For example, DHS uses data the LDP Office collects to measure progress against two goals established in the *DHS Workforce Strategy for Fiscal Years 2011-2016*. We agree that data collected to track the measures may provide information for measuring progress against some department-wide goals established in strategy documents; however, it is not evident how these or other LDP performance measures link to goals specific to the LDP.

We have previously found that linkages between goals and measures are most effective when they are clearly communicated to all staff within the agency so that everyone understands what the organization is trying to

---

[44]DHS, *DHS Learning Evaluation Guide*.

achieve.[45] Explicitly identifying program goals, creating an evident link between performance measures and program goals, and clearly communicating the linkage could help ensure that the behaviors and incentives created by the LDP's 12 performance measures support the LDP's intended outcomes, and that they are appropriate measures for the program.

- Clarity: Not all LDP performance measures possess clarity because some measures include terms that are ambiguous and for which the LDP Office has not documented definitions. For example, one of the LDP's measures is the percentage of developmental activities that fulfill LDP requirements delivered with shared resources. However, it is not clear what constitutes a "developmental activity" for the purpose of calculating this measure (e.g., a course or unit within a course), and the value could be different depending on the definition of "activity" used in the measure's calculation.[46] As a result, this measure could be confusing and misleading to users, such as DHS leadership and congressional constituents, by leading them to think that performance was better or worse than it actually was. According to the LDP Manager, the LDP Office has not documented definitions for terms used in its performance measures because components may elect to fulfill LDP requirements through varied approaches and this makes how terms such as "developmental activity" are defined contextually driven. While we recognize that components may use varied approaches to fulfilling LDP requirements, it is important that terms the LDP Office uses in its performances measures are clear so that users understand what the measures mean. LDP officials also stated that components are able to contact the LDP Office with questions about how to calculate the measures, and that the LDP Office will work with components to provide any requested clarification. Providing support to components is a positive step, but documenting definitions for ambiguous terms used in the measures could help ensure the meaning of their values is clear to stakeholders.
- Targets: The LDP's performance measures do not have measurable targets. According to the LDP Manager, the LDP has not set targets for

---

[45]GAO-03-143.

[46]LDP Office guidance establishes that developmental activities can include various learning modalities, including classroom and online training, reading, mentoring, coaching, experiential learning, resource kits, and other materials. However, the guidance does not explain how such activities should be delineated or quantified to calculate this measure.

its 12 program performance measures because it is too early in the process, as LDP officials have just established a baseline with fiscal year 2013 data. The LDP Manager anticipates developing LDP targets in the future and stated that program officials will consider doing so once they collect more data. The LDP Office does not have a definitive plan or time frame for setting targets, but according to the LDP Manager, expects to do so using fiscal year 2014 data. We agree that, consistent with key attributes of performance measures, developing measurable targets could help DHS determine whether the program's performance is meeting expectations. To set appropriate targets, however, it will be important for the LDP Office to first clearly identify program goals and ensure its performance measures link to the goals.

DHS leadership has previously identified implementation of leader development programs as important to the department's success and a means by which to improve its human capital management. For example, in February 2012, the then deputy secretary of homeland security stated that leader development is critical to DHS's growth and long-term success and must be a strategic mission investment priority. In addition, DHS has identified implementation of the LDP among the actions it is taking to address DHS's high-risk designation with respect to human capital management. By clearly identifying program goals and ensuring LDP performance measures include key attributes, such as linkage, clarity, and measurable targets, the LDP could strengthen its performance measurement, consequently producing actionable information for LDP management to use in identifying the need for, and making, program improvements.

Conclusions

As DHS faces increasingly complex national security challenges, it is important that it support employees with effective training and development programs to meet its mission requirements. Evaluating training and development programs is important for ensuring that such programs are cost-effective and continue to be relevant for the department. By updating DHS components' documented training evaluation processes to more fully address key attributes for effective training evaluation, DHS components could have better assurance that the components have more complete information to guide their efforts in conducting effective evaluations. Such documentation can further help ensure that processes for assessing whether training programs support component and DHS needs are repeatable and consistently implemented. Further, given limited budgetary resources, by identifying existing challenges that prevent DHS from accurately capturing its training costs department-wide and, to the extent that the benefits exceed the costs, implementing corrective measures to overcome these challenges, DHS could improve its awareness about the actual costs of its training programs, and enhance its ability to consistently and reliably capture training costs DHS-wide, thereby enhancing its resource stewardship.

In addition, DHS is in the process of implementing a department-wide leader development program to build leadership skills across all staff levels. The effectiveness of this program is particularly important given that DHS leadership has identified leader development as critical to the department's success. As DHS begins to assess the impact of the LDP program, clearly identifying LDP goals and ensuring that LDP performance measures possess key attributes, including (1) linkage to the program's goals, (2) clarity, and (3) measurable targets by which to assess the measures could help provide DHS with the actionable information it needs to identify and make program improvements.

Recommendations for Executive Action

To ensure effective evaluation of federal training programs and enhance DHS's stewardship of resources for federal training programs, we recommend that the Secretary of Homeland Security take the following two actions:

- direct DHS components to ensure that their documented training evaluation processes fully address attributes for effective training evaluation processes as they are drafted, updated, or revised and
- identify existing challenges that prevent DHS from accurately capturing training costs department-wide and, to the extent that the benefits of addressing those challenges exceed the costs, implement corrective measures to overcome these challenges.

In addition, to produce actionable information for DHS's LDP management to use in identifying the need for, and making, program improvements, we recommend that the Secretary of Homeland Security direct the Chief Human Capital Officer to clearly identify LDP goals and ensure LDP performance measures include key attributes, such as linkage, clarity, and measurable targets.

Agency Comments and Our Evaluation

We provided a draft of this report to DHS for review and comment. DHS provided written comments, which are reprinted in appendix IV, and technical comments, which we incorporated as appropriate. DHS agreed with all three of the recommendations and outlined steps to address them. If fully implemented, these actions will address the intent of our recommendations.

- With respect to the first recommendation, DHS agreed to ensure that effective training evaluation processes are documented and in place at components by incorporating a review of component training evaluation documents into the DHS Chief Human Capital Officer's audit of human resource functions. DHS reports that a full review of components should be completed with the fiscal year 2019 audit cycle.

- Regarding the second recommendation, DHS agreed to resolve the issue of capturing training costs Department-wide. For example, DHS plans to establish a team jointly chaired by the DHS Chief Human Capital Officer and the Chief Financial Officer, and comprised of representatives from both financial and training offices of each operational component and headquarters, that is to deliver a methodology to track and report training costs across DHS by June 30, 2015. DHS anticipates the new methodology will be implemented across all components by January 31, 2016.

- In response to the third recommendation, DHS agreed to publish clear DHS Leader Development Program goals and performance measures that include key attributes, such as linkage, clarity and measurable targets on the DHS intranet website by December 31, 2014.

We are sending copies of this report to appropriate congressional committees and the Secretary of Homeland Security. In addition, the report is available at no charge on the GAO website at http://www.gao.gov.

Should you or your staff have any questions concerning this report, please contact me at (202) 512-9627 or by e-mail at maurerd@gao.gov. Contact points for our Offices of Congressional Relations and Public Affairs may be found on the last page of this report. Key contributors to this report are listed in appendix VI.

Sincerely yours,

David Maurer
Director, Homeland Security and Justice

Appendix I: Objectives, Scope, and Methodology

Our objectives for this report were to address the following questions:

1. To what extent does the Department of Homeland Security (DHS) have documented processes to evaluate training and development programs and reliably capture costs?

2. What leader development programs has DHS implemented, what are stakeholders' perspectives on them, and to what extent does DHS measure program performance?

To understand training programs at DHS, we obtained information from the DHS Office of the Chief Human Capital Officer (OCHCO), and five selected components: the Federal Law Enforcement Training Center (FLETC), U.S. Customs and Border Protection (CBP), U.S. Immigration and Customs Enforcement (ICE), the Transportation Security Administration (TSA), and the United States Coast Guard. We selected these components to represent different DHS mission areas, workforce sizes, training costs, and number of career Senior Executive Service (SES) personnel. In addition, these components have a mix of new and more established training programs. When examining training programs at selected components, we reviewed component-level training evaluation and strategic plans when available; training budget requests; cost and expenditure documents; training procedures, policies, and organizational charts; and policies for identifying and prioritizing training programs; selected training course materials, and other relevant documents. To further our understanding of training at the component level, we also interviewed training officials at each of the selected components and identified these individuals based on their knowledge, experience, and leadership roles. We conducted our interviews at component headquarters located in the Washington, D.C. area, or field offices. In addition, as part of our review of DHS's delivery of mission-critical law enforcement training across components, we observed training at FLETC's Glynco, Georgia facilities. The perspectives DHS OCHCO and the selected components provided are not generalizable to all of DHS, but provided helpful insights into the selected components specific training and development programs at DHS.

To address the first question, regarding the extent to which DHS has documented processes to evaluate training and development programs, and ensure training costs are reliably captured, we reviewed DHS and component-specific documents and interviewed relevant officials at DHS OCHCO and each of the components. Specifically,

- To determine the extent to which DHS has documented processes to evaluate its training and development programs, we reviewed policies and procedures related to the evaluation of training programs, such as component-specific standard operating procedures and training development standards. We then assessed the documented processes from each of the selected components against attributes of training evaluation processes identified by the Office of Personnel Management (OPM), DHS, and GAO to determine the extent to which the documents include selected attributes of evaluation processes. We selected the attributes for our analysis to include attributes that were consistently identified in relevant criteria documents related to training evaluation, such as the *DHS Learning Evaluation Guide,*[1] the OPM *Training Evaluation Field Guide,*[2] and GAO's prior work on training and development, specifically the *Guide for Strategic Training and Development Efforts in the Federal Government.*[3] These attributes also align with those identified in *Standards for Internal Control in the Federal Government,* which calls for agencies to document the plans, methods, and procedures used to achieve missions, goals, and objectives and support performance-based management practices.[4] From these sources, we identified six attributes of a training evaluation process to conduct our analysis: (1) establishes goals about what the training program is supposed to achieve, (2) indicates which training programs are being evaluated, (3) explains the methodology used to conduct the evaluation, (4) presents time frames for conducting the evaluation, (5) presents roles and responsibilities for evaluation efforts, and (6) explains how the evaluation results will be used. We assessed each component's documented evaluation process to determine the extent to which the attributes were included and gave a component a rating indicating that the attribute was fully met, a component partially met the attribute but did not fully or consistently meet all parts, or the component did not include any information to meet the attribute. We also conducted semistructured interviews with officials responsible for conducting training evaluation at

---

[1]DHS, *DHS Learning Evaluation Guide* (Washington, D.C.: October 2010).

[2]OPM, *Training Evaluation Field Guide: Demonstrating the Value of Training at Every Level,* (Washington, D.C.: January 2011).

[3]GAO, *Human Capital: A Guide for Assessing Strategic Training and Development Efforts in the Federal Government,* GAO-04-546G (Washington, D.C.: March 2004).

[4]GAO, *Standards for Internal Control in the Federal Government* (Washington, D.C.: Nov. 1, 1999).

each of the five components to understand the evaluation process that
each component follows and how evaluation feedback is used.

- To assess the extent to which DHS ensures training costs are reliably
  captured, we reviewed information and relevant documentation on
  processes and steps components took to examine available budget and
  cost information. We further reviewed documentation on the process of
  capturing training costs from each of our selected components, including
  financial audit reports. As part of our review of cost tracking at DHS, we
  observed methods components used for identifying efficiencies in training
  to identify cost savings and employ more cost-effective alternatives. We
  also conducted semistructured interviews with DHS and component
  officials responsible for administering training programs and tracking
  costs to understand how DHS and components identified and captured
  costs, and any challenges they may have in doing so in a reliable
  manner. Through our review of cost-saving documentation and interviews
  with DHS and component officials, we sought illustrative examples to
  understand how OCHCO and the selected DHS components identified
  potential efficiencies and steps planned or already taken to achieve them.
  Accordingly, OCHCO and DHS component officials identified examples
  of cost savings realized in selected training programs from fiscal year
  2011 through fiscal year 2013, and we reviewed the reliability of the
  related cost-saving estimates. For example, we interviewed
  knowledgeable officials who provided cost estimates, reviewed the
  estimates related to cost savings, and replicated cost-saving calculations
  provided by components, including estimates for training equipment,
  salaries, and benefits. We determined through analysis of cost-saving
  estimates and interviews with knowledgeable officials at DHS and the
  selected components that the cost-saving data provided and reported for
  the illustrative examples in this product were sufficiently reliable for the
  purposes of illustrating the types of cost efficiencies that may be
  achieved. The cost-saving examples DHS OCHCO and components
  provided are not generalizable to all of DHS, but provided helpful insights
  into cost-saving efforts identified to date at DHS.

To address the second question, about leader development programs
DHS has implemented, we reviewed program documentation, analyzed
participant data, and interviewed officials from OCHCO and the selected
components.

- In particular, to determine what leader development programs DHS has
  implemented, we reviewed OCHCO Leader Development Program (LDP)
  curricula and requirements documentation, such as the *Senior Executive
  Service Candidate Development Program Candidate Guide* and *The*

Cornerstone Program Requirements and Accountability Guide, and
documentation of leader development programs provided by the selected
components, such as program descriptions and evaluations.[5] In addition,
we obtained and analyzed data from OCHCO and the selected
components on the number of participants in the leader development
programs they provided during fiscal years 2012 and 2013.[6] We
assessed the reliability of these data by interviewing agency officials
familiar with the sources of the data regarding internal controls built into
the information systems and stand-alone documents in which they are
stored and quality assurance steps performed after data are entered into
the systems or documents. In addition, we compared participant
completion data for the Fundamentals of DHS Leadership segment of the
Cornerstone Program—one of DHS's leader development programs—for
similar time periods that components provided to us and had previously
reported to the LDP Office. Where we identified discrepancies, we
interviewed officials to determine their cause and the correct values. We
determined that the data were sufficiently reliable for the purpose of
reporting the approximate number of program participants. We also
interviewed officials from OCHCO and the components regarding
implemented and planned leader development programs.

- To determine officials' perspectives on DHS leader development
  programs, we obtained OCHCO and component officials' views on the
  development and implementation of leader development programs and
  the programs' strengths and weaknesses. The perspectives the
  interviewees provided are not generalizable to all DHS officials, but
  provided helpful insights into strengths and weaknesses of leader
  development programs.
- To assess the extent to which DHS measures the performance of leader
  development programs, we reviewed program documentation from
  OCHCO and the selected components, including performance
  measurement requirements and guidance. In addition, we interviewed
  cognizant officials about what performance measurement information
  they collect and how they use the information. Through these efforts, we

---

[5]DHS Leader Development Program, *Senior Executive Service Candidate Development
Program Candidate Guide* (Washington, D.C) and DHS Leader Development Program,
The Cornerstone Program Requirements and Accountability Guide (Washington, D.C:
2013).

[6]We selected this time frame in order to focus on the most current leader development
programs DHS provides. Fiscal year 2013 was the most recent year for which complete
data were available at the time of our review.

determined that the LDP Office uses 12 performance measures to assess the LDP's impact. We assessed these measures against three of nine selected key attributes for performance measures identified in prior GAO work that we identified as relevant given the maturity level of the LDP.[7] In particular, given that the LDP is a relatively new program, we focused our analysis on three attributes that we identified as foundational and—having linkage with division- and agency-wide goals, being clear, and having measurable targets. We selected linkage because aligning measures with division- and agency-wide goals and mission helps ensure that the behaviors and incentives created by the measures support the division- or agency-wide goals or mission. Once the measures' relevance to a program is ensured through linkage, then assessment of more detailed aspects of the measures, such as reliability, is more relevant. Similarly, we selected having measurable targets because, without measurable targets, it may not be evident whether performance is meeting expectations. With regard to clarity, if a measure is not clearly stated and the name and definition are not consistent with the methodology used to calculate it, performance data could be confusing and misleading to users, such as department leadership and congressional constituents.

We conducted this performance audit from July 2013 to September 2014, in accordance with generally accepted government auditing standards. Those standards require that we plan and perform the audit to obtain sufficient, appropriate evidence to provide a reasonable basis for our findings and conclusions based on our audit objectives. We believe that the evidence obtained provides a reasonable basis for our findings and conclusions based on our audit objectives.

---

[7]GAO, *Tax Administration: IRS Needs to Further Refine Its Tax Filing Season Performance Measures*, GAO-03-143 (Washington, D. C.: Nov. 22, 2002). GAO developed these nine attributes of performance goals and measures based on previously established GAO criteria, consideration of key legislation, and review of performance management literature. In GAO-03-143, GAO applied the attributes to assess Internal Revenue Service performance measures. However, because the attributes are derived from sources generally applicable to performance measures, they are also relevant for assessing LDP performance measures.

Appendix II: Presence of Effective Training Attributes in DHS's Documented Training Evaluation Processes

Component	Establishes goals about what the training program is supposed to achieve	Indicates which programs are being evaluated	Explains methodology used to conduct the evaluation	Presents timeframes for conducting the evaluation	Presents agency roles and responsibilities for evaluation efforts	Explains how the evaluation results will be used
U.S. Customs and Border Protection (CBP)	●	●	◗[a]	◗[b]	◗[c]	●
U.S. Immigration and Customs Enforcement (ICE)	●	●.	●	●	◗[d]	●
Coast Guard	●	●	●	◗[e]	●	●
Transportation Security Administration (TSA)[f]	●	●	◗[g]	◗[h]	◗[i]	●
Federal Law Enforcement Training Center (FLETC)	●	●	◗[j]	●	●	●

●: The component's documented evaluation processes fully included information to meet the attr bute for all aspects of its evaluation process.

◗: The component's documented evaluation processes included some information to address a given attr bute but did not include information to fully and consistently meet all parts of the attribute. This includes, for example, incomplete evaluation processes or incomplete information to address a given attr bute for certain levels of the evaluation.

○: The component's documented evaluation processes did not include information to address the attr bute for the evaluation process.

Source: GAO analysis of documented evaluation processes. I GAO-14-688

[a]CBP's documentation presents ways CBP can implement the Kirkpatrick model but does not indicate the actual process that will be used.

[b]CBP's documentation outlines when the various levels of evaluations are supposed to be administered, but does not present a timeframe for CBP to analyze the evaluation feedback.

[c]CBP's documentation identifies some CBP entities that perform the evaluations and receive the evaluation information, but does not do so consistently for each level of evaluation.

[d]ICE's documentation outlines who is responsible for the various level 1 evaluation activities and what ICE stakeholders should be involved in the process, but does not provide this information consistently for evaluation levels 2 and 3.

[e]The Coast Guard's documentation provides guidance on when to administer the evaluation surveys, but it does not specify timeframes for the Coast Guard to analyze the evaluation data.

[f]The documentation that we reviewed for TSA includes the draft Training Development Standards that will be applicable to all TSA training programs. For this analysis, we excluded the evaluation processes that are specific to Federal Air Marshal Service training programs alone because they are governed by separate evaluation processes to retain FLETA accreditation that do not apply to other aspects of training at TSA.

[g]TSA's documentation states that it will evaluate training programs using the Kirkpatrick model and discusses the process in a very general sense. However, the documentation does not indicate

specifically how TSA will conduct each level of evaluation or the circumstances in which a certain approach will be used.

[h]TSA's documentation outlines when it will administer each evaluation; however, it does not discuss timeframes for analyzing evaluation data.

[i]The document indicates that TSA's Office of Training and Workforce Engagement (OTWE) conducts evaluation activities. However, the document does not spell out the roles and responsibilities for the evaluation activities within OTWE, which is the office respons ble for training overall at TSA, not just evaluations.

[j]FLETC's documentation indicates that it will evaluate its training programs using the four-level Kirkpatrick model. However, the documents do not consistently indicate how FLETC will develop, administer, and analyze the evaluation data for each level. For example, for level 3 evaluations, FLETC's documentation includes some policies and procedures that govern the evaluations, but these procedures do not provide specifics on the process such as how the surveys are developed and deployed, and how the surveys are sent to a sample of students, among others.

The following information appears as interactive content in figure 3 in the report body when viewed electronically.

Table 10: Leader Development Framework—Programs and Implementation Status, as of August 2014

Tier	Component program(s)	Description	Program development/implementation status
Executive	Capstone	Capstone is a 3-week program administered by the Leader Development Program (LDP) Office that includes discussion forums, operational site visits and learning activities intended to address real-world strategic issues. Moving forward the LDP Office plans to develop and incorporate additional components identified by the Leader Development Framework focusing on crisis leadership, executive coaching, and continuous development.	Program implementation underway. The LDP Office piloted the first Capstone cohort in summer 2012. The second cohort was delayed due to sequestration, but delivery began in March 2014. The LDP Office plans to begin developing requirements for the additional Capstone components in fiscal year 2015.
Manager	Keystone	Keystone is to consist of three components focusing on (1) transitioning to management positions, (2) building capability to lead with interagency perspective, and (3) managers as mentors and coaches and the interagency in action.	Program not developed or implemented. The LDP Office plans to begin development in fiscal year 2014 and implement the program in fiscal year 2015.
Supervisor	Cornerstone	Cornerstone consists of a set of baseline requirements intended to provide DHS components with a developmental roadmap for new and seasoned supervisors. DHS components are required to meet these requirements and may do so through their existing training, new developmental activities, collaborative cross-component programming, or a combination. Cornerstone includes requirements that span four areas • Understanding the DHS Leadership Commitment: classroom and online instruction to communicate expectations, roles, challenges, and rewards of supervision to those wishing to consider the supervisory path; • Supervisory Onboarding: in-person or virtual classroom training for new DHS supervisors at any level to increase their understanding of a supervisor's roles and duties, among other things; 8 hours of mentoring from a seasoned supervisor; and individual exercises, such as completion of a checklist that includes various tasks. • Fundamentals of DHS Leadership: 40 hours of instruction for all federal first-time supervisors spanning various competencies, such as team building and developing others; and • Continuous Supervisory Leader Development: 12 hours of development and 12 hours of "give-back," or contributing to the development of others (e.g., through mentoring or teaching) annually.	Program implemented. DHS components began Cornerstone implementation in fiscal year 2012 and most components completed significant implementation in fiscal year 2013.

Tier	Component program(s)	Description	Program development/implementation status
Team lead	Milestone	Milestone is to consist of development options for components to implement. These options are to focus on career coaching; team training; cross-component shadowing, mentoring, and exercises; and various experiential development opportunities.	Program development initiated. The LDP Office began development in fiscal year 2014. Component implementation is planned for fiscal year 2015.
Team member	Foundations	Foundations is to consist of development options for components to implement. These options are to focus on leading one's self, discipline-based curriculum and blended learning, technical expertise, and various experiential development opportunities.	Program development initiated. The LDP Office began development in fiscal year 2014. Component implementation is planned for fiscal year 2015.
Spans framework tiers	Senior Executive Service Candidate Development Program (CDP)	CDP is an 18- to24-month leadership development program administered by the LDP Office and intended to develop a cadre of leaders ready to fill executive positions. The program includes, among other things • completion of a 360-degree assessment used to identify competency gaps with respect to Executive Core Qualifications (ECQ) required by the Office of Personnel Management (OPM) for appointment to the Senior Executive Service; • development of a plan with a Senior Executive Service mentor to address identified ECQ gaps; • courses that address individual ECQ gaps and general skills needed to succeed as a homeland security executive; and 6-to 8-month developmental assignments at the executive level.	Program implemented (pre-existing program). The LDP Office launched the first cohort in summer 2011. The second cohort commenced in summer 2013. The LDP is recruiting participants for the third cohort.
	DHS Fellows	DHS Fellows is intended to prepare DHS leaders selected throughout the department who are committed to bringing a joint perspective to leading people and the mission in a variety of disciplines. DHS Fellows consists of a10-month curriculum that includes site visits, residential sessions, coaching, instruction, and a 60-to 90-day rotational assignment.	Program implemented (preexisting program). There have been seven DHS Fellows cohorts, the first of which was launched in 2007. The sixth cohort was launched in spring 2012, and the seventh cohort commenced in spring 2013. The LDP Office is redesigning this program, after which it plans to launch the eighth cohort in spring 2015.

Source: GAO analysis of DHS information. I GAO-14-688.

The Department of Homeland Security's (DHS) Leader Development Program (LDP) Office has developed a program-wide assessment approach intended to analyze the impact of the LDP over time and to assess whether the program is targeting the right things in the right way. This assessment approach, which applies to all LDP program elements—including Capstone, Cornerstone, and other programs—consists of (1) biannually collecting and analyzing completion rate data, (2) collecting and analyzing responses to six core evaluation questions, and (3) tracking 12 program performance measures. Table 11 provides more detailed information about this approach.

Table 11: Summary of Department of Homeland Security (DHS) Leader Development Program (LDP) Assessment Approach

Assessment element	Description
Biannually collect and analyze completion rate data for all LDP programs implemented by components to track progress against *DHS Workforce Strategy for Fiscal Years 2011-2016* targets.[a]	The *DHS Workforce Strategy for Fiscal Years 2011-2016* includes two performance measures with targets related to the LDP. These are • the percentage of employees completing a DHS-wide leadership development program offering and • the percentage of supervisors that have completed mandatory annual supervisory training.
Collect and analyze responses to six core evaluation questions administered immediately following each developmental activity and 6 months later.	Participants are to respond to the following statements using a five-point scale (e.g., agree, disagree, etc.): • The format (classroom, online, reading, etc.) of this developmental activity was conducive to my ability to apply knowledge on the job. • This developmental activity gave me knowledge or skills that I did not otherwise gain from on-the-job experience. • Applying the knowledge and skills from this developmental activity will make [has made] me more effective in leading DHS mission execution. • I consider this developmental activity to be [have been] a worthwhile investment. • I would recommend [have recommended] this developmental activity to a colleague at my leader level. • I have [have had] the support of my supervisor in applying what I have learned back on the job.

Assessment element	Description
Track 12 program performance measures.	The measures are • Six-month follow-up participant feedback rating on core evaluation question "The format (classroom, online, reading, etc.) of this developmental activity was conducive to my ability to apply knowledge on the job" • Immediate participant feedback rating on core evaluation question "I would recommend this developmental activity to a colleague at my leader level" • Immediate participant feedback rating on core evaluation question "This developmental activity gave me knowledge or skills that I did not otherwise gain from on-the-job experience" • Percentage of onboard Senior Executive Service Candidate Development Program-certified graduates who are eligible to be placed in an Senior Executive Service position within the department • Number of participants in "Understanding the DHS Leadership Commitment" online or in-person offerings • Percentage of developmental activities that fulfill LDP requirements that consist of cross-component participation • Percentage of developmental activities that fulfill LDP requirements delivered with shared resources • Overall "Best Places to Work" in the federal government ranking[b] • Number of employee-driven supervisor nominations for leadership awards • Effective Leadership ranking on "Best Places to Work" • Six-month follow-up participant feedback rating on core evaluation question "I consider this developmental activity to have been a worthwhile investment" • Six-month follow-up participant feedback rating on core evaluation question "Applying the knowledge and skills from this developmental activity has made me more effective leading DHS mission execution"

Source: GAO analysis of DHS information. I GAO-14-688

[a]The *DHS Workforce Strategy for Fiscal Years 2011-2016* is intended to address programs and resources to support DHS employees and advance the department's capabilities in the areas of recruitment, retention, and employee development.

[b]The Best Places to Work ranking is published by the Partnership for Public Service and is derived from results of the Office of Personnel Management's Federal Employee Viewpoint Survey (FEVS)— a tool that measures employees' perceptions of whether and to what extent conditions characterizing successful organizations are present in their agency. In particular, according to the Partnership for Public Service, the Best Places to Work ranking is based on employee responses to three FEVS assessment items: (1) I recommend my organization as a good place to work. (2) Considering everything, how satisfied are you with your job? (3) Considering everything, how satisfied are you with your organization?

U.S. Department of Homeland Security
Washington, DC 20528

Homeland Security

August 21, 2014

David Maurer
Director, Homeland Security and Justice
U.S. Government Accountability Office
441 G Street, NW
Washington, DC 20548

Re: Draft Report GAO 14-688, "DHS TRAINING: Improved Documentation, Resource Tracking and Performance Measurement Could Strengthen Efforts"

Dear Mr. Maurer:

Thank you for the opportunity to review and comment on this draft report. The U.S. Department of Homeland Security (DHS) appreciates the U.S. Government Accountability Office's (GAO's) work in planning and conducting its review and issuing this report.

DHS is pleased to note GAO's recognition that the Department has processes in place to evaluate training, track resources, and assess leader development. Specifically, the draft report noted that the U.S. Customs and Border Protection, the Federal Law Enforcement Training Center (FLETC), the U.S. Immigration and Customs Enforcement, the Transportation Security Administration, and the U.S. Coast Guard all reflected a number of attributes of an effective training evaluation process in their documentation, and that the DHS Office of the Chief Human Capital Officer's (OCHCO's) Leader Development Program (LDP) Office developed a program-wide assessment approach to analyze the impact of the LDP.

The draft report contained three recommendations with which the Department concurs. Specifically, GAO recommended that the Secretary of Homeland Security:

Recommendation 1: Direct DHS components to ensure that their documented training evaluation processes fully address attributes for effective training evaluation processes as they are drafted, updated, or revised.

Response: Concur. To ensure that Components fully address attributes for effective training evaluation in their documentation, OCHCO will review Component training evaluation documents during Human Resource Operations Audits (HROAs). The HROAs include a review of training evaluation documentation to ensure effective evaluation processes are in place. Each Component's human resources function is audited every four years. OCHCO will develop a plan for evaluation to begin with HROAs scheduled in the fiscal year (FY) 2016 audit cycle. A full review of Components should be completed with the FY 2019 audit cycle. The FLETC review will be limited to training provided to FLETC employees. Estimated Completion Date (ECD): September 30, 2019.

Recommendation 2: Identify existing challenges that prevent DHS from accurately capturing training costs department-wide and, to the extent that the benefits of addressing those challenges exceed the costs, implement corrective measures to overcome these challenges.

Response: Concur. A team, jointly chaired by both DHS's Chief Human Capital and Chief Financial Officers and comprised of representatives from both financial and training offices of each operational Component and headquarters, will be charged with solving the issue of capturing training costs. The team will build on GAO's recommendations and observations within this report and deliver a methodology to track and report training costs applicable across DHS by June 30, 2015. Implementation of the new methodology will begin immediately and will be in place in all Components by the start of the 2016 calendar year. ECD: January 31, 2016.

Recommendation 3: Direct the Chief Human Capital Officer to clearly identify LDP goals and ensure LDP performance measures include key attributes, such as linkage, clarity, and measurable targets.

Response: Concur. The LDP Office will deliver a draft document clearly identifying LDP goals and demonstrating linkage, clarity, and measureable targets for LDP performance measures to the DHS Chief Learning Officer by September 30, 2014, for review. Upon final approval by the DHS Chief Human Capital Officer, the DHS Chief Learning Officer will post this document to the DHS Connect Intranet LDP page. ECD: December 31, 2014.

Again, thank you for the opportunity to review and comment on this draft report. Technical comments were previously provided under separate cover. Please feel free to contact me if you have any questions. We look forward to working with you in the future.

Sincerely,

Jim H. Crumpacker, CIA, CFE
Director
Departmental GAO-OIG Liaison Office

2

Appendix VI: GAO Contact and Staff Acknowledgments

GAO Contact	David C. Maurer, (202) 512-9627 or maurerd@gao.gov
Staff Acknowledgments	In addition to the contact named above, Joseph P. Cruz, Assistant Director; Chuck Bausell; Gary Bianchi; Gustavo Crosetto; Peter DelToro; Michele Fejfar; Eric Hauswirth; Adam Hoffman; Susan Hsu; Kirk Kiester; Tracey King; Taylor Matheson; Signora May; Linda Miller; Julia Vieweg; and Yee Wong made key contributions to this report.